HOW TO BAKE

HOW TO B

PAUL HOLLYWOOD

Photography by Peter Cassidy

BLOOMSBURY
LONDON · NEW DELHI · NEW YORK · SYDNEY

INTRODUCTION

I have been passionate about baking since I was eight years old. My father was a baker and I spent a lot of time in his shops as I was growing up, helping with jobs such as jamming the doughnuts and filling scones with cream. I loved to see the professionals at work. I was intrigued by the way a baker would take a few simple raw materials and create a beautiful and delicious finished product from them. To me, watching the kneading of dough was almost hypnotic. That fascination is with me to this day. I have been baking for thirty years now and I've never wanted to do anything else.

When I was seventeen I was let loose 'on the tables' where the loaves and pastries were formed, before learning the correct way to bake all the breads, pastries and cakes that we sold. After serving this apprenticeship with my dad, I moved on to manage my own shop, then to work in the kitchens of various establishments – including The Dorchester, Cliveden and the Chester Grosvenor, as well as restaurants on the Continent – honing my skills all the time.

I have learnt a great deal over the last three decades – not just the best, simplest ways to do things, but the worst ways too. I've seen hard-won, age-old skills consigned to the scrap heap and traditional techniques replaced with modern, cost-cutting methods that save time but sacrifice flavour and quality. I have never stopped loving baking though, nor lost faith in the truly passionate bakers of this country, whether they are professionals or home cooks.

That is why, in this book, I want to celebrate the really great breads and pastries and show you how to make them. Many accomplished cooks will try any number of new recipes, yet balk at the idea of turning out a loaf of bread or a brioche because they think it is difficult or complicated. It's not. All kinds of myths and mysteries have evolved around this branch of cookery over the years and a lot of them are utter nonsense. Yes, there are pitfalls to be avoided, and useful tricks of the trade to be learnt, but once you've mastered the basic techniques, you can become a great baker.

My book covers a whole range of different breads as well as pastries and irresistible cakes, biscuits and puddings. As a professional, I have had the time to really work at each part of the baking process: time to play, invent and experiment, and the benefit of that experience is in this step-by-step guide. Each recipe has an in-depth method that shows my way of doing things, enabling you to create something perfect. In effect, I will be there with you in your kitchen, guiding you through the process and solving problems before they happen. You will discover that you can, very easily, create breads, tarts and cakes at home that look every bit as good as those you'll buy in the shops – and taste better.

Successful baking is about having the appropriate kit and ingredients, and understanding the techniques. I am very particular about using the right tool for the job – if the knife I need or the tin I want is not to hand I've been known to get pretty irate! Finding the best ingredients, the ones you feel most comfortable using, is important too. If you put rubbish in, you'll get rubbish out. But don't be deterred by any of this. Sourcing the best ingredients and equipment is not hard (see Directory, page 298).

You'll find recipes here for baked goods from all over the world, from Continental couronne, fougasse and strudel, tartes and croissants, to Indian chapatis and Middle Eastern maneesh. But I want to celebrate our own tradition of baking too. This country has some wonderful basic breads that can rival the French baguette or the Italian focaccia: breads such as the cottage loaf, barm cake or bloomer. Yes, a really well-made bloomer is a great thing.

The way we bake has changed so much in recent decades: it's too focused on speed and making a profit. Commercial bakers no longer take the time to let their doughs ferment slowly, which creates flavour, and many home bakers don't either. Yet, if you find that time (and most of it is not hands-on work time), and give a little attention to detail, then I guarantee you can create breads, cakes and other bakes that your family and friends will love.

I've given plenty of information in the introduction to each chapter because a little bit of knowledge goes a long way in baking. If, in addition to knowing how to bake a loaf of bread or a custard tart, you understand why you do things in a certain way, then you will be well-equipped to begin your own baking adventure. I want to send you off into your own world of baking where, because you understand the simple chemistry and basic techniques, you can experiment and create your own delicious versions of the recipes I'm sharing with you here. My advice is always to take your time, and to treat any mishap as an opportunity to learn.

I am as passionate about baking today as when I was that young lad, watching my dad at work. I still love the feeling I get from manipulating good raw ingredients into something fantastic. I hope I can pass that on to you and help you to create a little bit of magic in your own kitchen.

GETTING STARTED WITH

HERE I WILL BE explaining the key ingredients and basic procedures behind all bread-making. The process is not difficult or complex but, in order to produce really good results, you do need to make sure you have good-quality ingredients and, where necessary, some basic items of kit. You must also understand the techniques and why they work. I'm going to show you how to mix a good, soft dough, which invariably produces a better bread than a firm dough, and how to judge when that dough has been kneaded sufficiently.

Bread-making is an acquired skill and practice makes perfect. Over the years I have evolved my own techniques in both kneading and shaping, which I will guide you through. My recipes are tried and tested. If you want to tweak any of them, then go ahead, once you have mastered the basics.

All of the breads in this book are best eaten within 24 hours of baking but they will keep for a couple of days in a bread bin and are perfectly acceptable if you refresh them in a hot oven at 220°C for 5 minutes before eating. Alternatively, they can be frozen, defrosted at room temperature and then refreshed, as above.

INGREDIENTS

There are just five simple key ingredients in bread-making: flour, yeast, salt, fat and water, with various options, particularly in the choice of flour.

FLOUR

Semolina (1), spelt flour (2), malted bread flour (3), strong white bread flour (4), rye flour (5), strong wholemeal bread flour (6), plain white flour (7).

Bread needs 'strong' flour, which means one with a protein level above 12 per cent. For cakes or biscuits, you need flour with a lower protein level, below 12 per cent. The protein level indicates how much gluten there is in the flour: gluten being the 'glue' that binds the dough together and creates structure. High-gluten flours give the chewy texture you want in a bread, whereas low-gluten flours give a crumbly texture.

Start with a white bread flour, as it is the easiest to use. Once you find one you like – and this shouldn't be difficult as most supermarkets sell good-quality bread flour – stick with it. Do bear in mind that, however accurate a recipe is, each brand of flour will absorb a slightly different amount of water, depending on its precise protein level. Generally, good-quality flour will take more water, a lower grade of flour less. So, when you start making bread, keep with your chosen flour and adjust your recipes, noting how much water that particular flour needs to get the right texture.

There are lots of flours on the market suitable for making bread. I particularly like Marriage's, Waitrose Organic, Doves Farm and Wright's flours (see Directory, page 298).

Strong white bread flour PROTEIN LEVEL 11–13 PER CENT
Until recently, most millers blended British flour, which typically has a protein level of 11–13 per cent, with Canadian flour, which has a higher content. This was because the baking industry demanded very high-protein flour that would give bread a 'bloom' or 'spring' in the oven. Also, as the flour absorbed more water, bakers would get a better yield and more profit from it. However, many millers in this country now use purely British flour.

Plain white flour PROTEIN LEVEL 9–11 PER CENT
Also known as 'cake flour', this is used for cakes, biscuits, crackers and most pastry, as well as soda bread. It is also sometimes mixed with strong flour in a bread recipe, to produce a slightly softer crumb. Unlike bread flour, plain flour should not be overworked or it will become rubbery. Avoid this by gently massaging the mixture or dough, not pummelling it.

Stoneground strong wholemeal bread flour PROTEIN LEVEL 12 PER CENT
This makes delicious bread and it is one of my favourites. Wholemeal flour retains all the best bits of the wheat kernel and therefore has a higher fibre and nutrient content. I choose stoneground wholemeal if possible: stone-grinding creates less heat than mechanical grinding, thereby preserving more nutrients in the grain. Wholemeal flours are more dense than white flours: they absorb more water and the dough requires more kneading. You can use wholemeal bread flour in biscuits and muffins; I suggest blending it with plain white flour to take the overall protein level below 12 per cent.

Malted bread flour PROTEIN LEVEL 10–11 PER CENT

This nutty-tasting flour, also known as 'Granary flour', has been popular since the 1970s. Although fairly dark in colour, it is essentially a white flour with added flakes of malted wheat. The protein level in malted flours can vary, and a bit more kneading is sometimes needed in order to develop the gluten and create a well-structured loaf. To be on the safe side, I always add an extra 5 minutes of kneading for a dough made with malted flour.

Spelt flour PROTEIN LEVEL 10 PER CENT

This well-flavoured flour has attracted a huge following recently. Its health benefits have been much publicised and some people with wheat intolerance find they can eat it without ill effects. Nevertheless, spelt is a type of wheat and contains gluten, albeit at a slightly lower level than some other wheat flours. It is not suitable for people with wheat allergy or coeliac disease. Because of the lower gluten level, dough made with spelt has a tendency to spread outwards while proving and baking, rather than springing upwards. I always encourage home bakers to bake spelt dough in a tin, which will only allow it to go in one direction (upwards), creating a more balanced loaf.

Rye flour PROTEIN LEVEL BELOW 10 PER CENT

Rye is a grass, different from wheat but related to it and it does contain some gluten. Rye flour has been widely used for bread-making for centuries but, as it is a 'weak' low-protein flour, it behaves differently from standard wheat flours. It's a little more difficult to work, making quite a heavy, sticky dough that takes longer to rise, but you can get delicious results with it.

Fine semolina

I don't use this to make the bread itself, but as a light coating that makes the soft dough easier to handle, and gives the finished loaf a lovely, crunchy crust. It is widely available but, if you can't get hold of it, using ordinary bread flour to coat the dough is absolutely fine.

YEAST

In Tudor Britain, most bakeries were situated next to brewers because this was the source of their yeast. The barm – the froth on top of the beers – would be scooped up by the baker and put into his dough to leaven the bread. However, this fairly acidic yeast created a very tangy, bitter loaf. In the late 1800s, the kind of commercial yeast we know today, which produces a much milder loaf, was introduced into bakeries.

For years, I used fresh yeast at my bakery. However, since converting to instant yeast – also called 'easy-blend' or 'fast-action' yeast – I've found no difference in the quality of my breads. Instant yeast is easy to buy and it stores well. It's what I always use at home too. I avoid standard dried yeast, which needs to be activated with water, as this simply creates more work. I like Doves Farm Quick Yeast because it comes loose in the pack so you can measure out exactly what you need: I find that 10g per 500g flour is just about right. This is a touch more than the 7g recommended on many instant yeast sachets, and it creates just that bit more fermentation in the dough, which adds to the flavour. If you can only get hold of 7g sachets, you can still weigh out the yeast of course, but it's fine just to use two of them (14g) for 500g flour. Bear in mind that instant yeast is a concentrate. If you want to use fresh yeast in any of my recipes, you will need 20 per cent more than the amount of instant yeast called for.

SALT

Salt is very important in a dough, not just because it prevents the bread from tasting dull and bland; it also strengthens the gluten in the mix. The salt I use to mix into a dough is common, fine-grained cooking salt. I use other salts for other jobs – sea salt flakes to top a focaccia, for example.

FAT

Fat is incorporated into bread to help it stay soft. You do not have to add fat to your dough but, if you want the crumb to stay tender for more than 24 hours, I certainly would. Whether you go for oil or butter is up to you. When making a basic white loaf, I would use very soft unsalted butter, but for an Italian-style bread, I choose olive oil.

WATER

Ordinary tap water is fine for bread-making. However, the temperature of the water you use is critical to producing a loaf with good texture and flavour. I use cool water – at around 15°C. If a recipe calls for 'tepid' water, I mean around 20°C. Older recipe books tell you to use warm water, which helps the dough rise quickly. It's true that adding warm water speeds up the whole baking process, but in doing so you will lose flavour. Slower-rising dough grows and forms pockets of carbon dioxide in exactly the same way, but as the fermentation process is longer, the bread will taste better. This is because as the yeast feeds on the flour it releases alcohol, while bacteria within the dough produce acids, both of which build flavour. The longer the fermentation, the deeper the flavour – hence the rich, tangy taste of slow-rising sourdoughs. I think of dough like a bottle of good red wine – you wouldn't drink it straight after bottling, it needs time to mature.

Incidentally, when I add milk to a dough, I do warm it up a little first. Milk, because it contains fat, actually retards the action of the yeast slightly and warming it helps to balance this out.

The amount of water listed in each recipe is a guide: you may find what you actually use deviates by up to 20ml either way. This is because different flours can vary significantly in the amount of water they absorb (see Flour, page 11–12). I add enough water to most of my doughs to make them really quite wet and sticky initially; this is as they should be.

TECHNIQUES

There are defined stages in bread-making: mixing, kneading, rising, knocking back, shaping, proving and baking, which call for specific techniques. None of these is difficult to master: practice makes perfect.

MIXING

The initial mixing of the dough takes place in a bowl. Put the flour(s) into your mixing bowl and mix them together roughly if you are using more than one type. Then add the salt to one side of the bowl (1) and add the yeast to the other side (2); this is important because the salt can kill the yeast if it comes into immediate contact with it. You don't have to mix the dry ingredients further at this stage.

Add the oil or butter to the bowl. Pour in most of the water (3) and start combining everything with the fingers of one hand, 'scrunching' the ingredients together, then stirring them round with your fingers and gradually incorporating the dry flour from the sides of the bowl. Add more water (4) until you have a soft dough and all the flour is mixed in. You are not looking for a thorough mixing at this stage – that will happen when you knead the dough – you just want to get the right amount of water into the flour. This is a really messy stage, as the dough will stick to your hands, but don't worry, it becomes much smoother and less sticky when kneaded.

In some cases, with a very wet or sticky dough, I recommend doing all the mixing and kneading in a mixer with a dough hook (see page 29). Generally, you can still work the dough by hand if you want to, but it will be fairly messy!

KNEADING

Kneading mixes the ingredients together thoroughly and is crucial for developing the gluten in the flour in order to create a smooth, elastic dough. There are no hard-and-fast rules – how you knead is up to you.

Start by learning how to simply fold the dough. Tuck the top into the middle ①, turn the dough 45° and repeat again and again. About 10 minutes of this repetitive action will give you a soft, malleable dough.

Or you can stretch the dough by pushing the top away from you ② then folding it back into the middle ③, turning it 45° and repeating over and over again for at least 5, more often 10 minutes, until the dough is smooth. You will see and feel the consistency of the dough changing during kneading. As the gluten develops, the dough will become smoother, more elastic and more cogent. It will be begin to hold together in a ball ④, rather than stick to you and the work surface, and it develops a soft, smooth skin. As you make more bread, you will get better at kneading and come to recognise that point when the dough has been worked enough.

You will find the consistency of many of my doughs, initially, to be pretty wet and sticky. This will give you lighter, more open-textured and altogether more delicious bread. As you knead, the dough will become less wet and sticky, but it should remain very soft. Kneading a soft dough takes a bit of confidence, but please persevere. If you add much less water than I suggest, or keep adding flour to the dough as you knead, you will end up with a stiff dough and a brick-like loaf of bread. That's why I generally advise that you use olive oil on your work surface, rather than flour. It will help you experience what the dough should feel like.

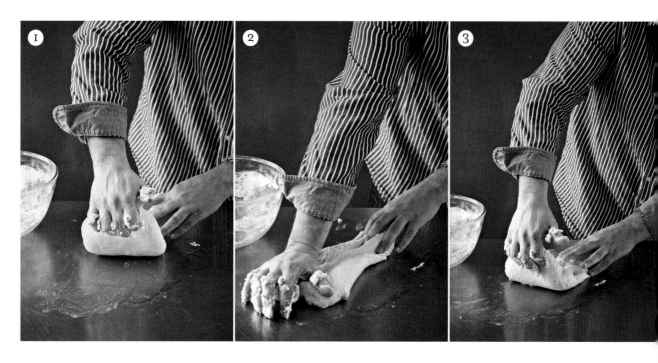

4

RISING

Once your dough has been mixed and kneaded, it needs to be left to rise until it has at least doubled in size and become bouncy and shiny. During this time the yeast feeds on the nutrients in the flour and produces bubbles of carbon dioxide, which cause the bread to rise. This initial rising stage should take between 1 and 2 hours at normal room temperature (20–22°C), but you can leave it for up to 3 hours; it doesn't matter if the dough trebles or even quadruples in size. Be patient and give it the time it needs to at least double. Rising is important and makes the dough easier to handle and shape.

With most doughs, I clean out the bowl it was mixed in, oil it very lightly with olive oil and return the kneaded dough to it for rising. Covering the bowl with cling film (1) or a tea towel protects the dough from draughts, which can cause a skin to form and inhibit rising. With very wet doughs, I use an oiled, 2–3 litre, square plastic container as they tend to rise a lot, but also because when you tip the dough out, it's already in a roughly square form, which makes it easier to shape. Sometimes I simply leave a wet dough to rise in the bowl of the electric mixer if I have used it.

It's worthwhile making a mark on the side of the bowl or container you put your dough in, and using it as an indicator of how much the dough has grown. Make a note of the degree of growth, time and temperature of your kitchen. This will help you to gauge timings next time you make bread.

When the dough has reached its maximum growth (2), crease marks will appear on top and it will begin to collapse and fall in on itself. We call this the 'drop-back'. The dough can be reformed and left to rise a second time if you wish: the yeast will continue to feed and release gas and the dough will swell again. The longer a loaf takes to rise, the better (see Water, page 13), though I would not allow a dough to rise more than three times, as its structure will begin to weaken and the growth will become sporadic.

KNOCKING BACK THE DOUGH

After this initial rising period, the dough usually needs to be 'knocked back' or deflated, so it is easy to handle and shape. Simply lift the dough out of the bowl (3) onto a lightly floured surface and fold it repeatedly in on itself until it is smooth and all the air has been knocked out of it (4). However, in some cases, rolling the dough out to a certain size or shape is the only knocking back you need. And with some very wet doughs, used to make particularly open-textured breads such as ciabatta, I don't knock back at all but handle the risen dough gently so as to keep the air trapped inside.

DIVIDING THE DOUGH

If you are making rolls or more than one loaf you will need to divide the dough. I use a Scotch scraper (see page 28) to do this. Alternatively, you can use a table knife. To ensure accuracy, use digital scales to weigh the dough, or simply judge by eye if you are comfortable to do so.

SHAPING THE DOUGH

Experimenting with different shapes is one of the many pleasures of baking your own bread, from a simple round cob or oval loaf to a neat bloomer or decorative plait.

Cob

This is the term used to describe a domed round loaf. If you are making bread for the first time, this is a good shape to start with.

To form a cob, first tip out your risen dough onto a very lightly floured surface, then knock out the air with your hands. Flatten the dough into a rough rectangle then roll it to into an oblong. Turn the dough so that the longer edge is running away from you and flatten it slightly (1). Now roll the two ends in towards the centre so you end up with a chunky, squarish shape (2). Turn the dough over on your work surface, so that the join is underneath (3).

To shape the dough into a smooth, domed cob, you now need to use both hands. With your palms turned upwards, position your hands on each side and slightly underneath the dough. Move your hands round the cob, tucking the dough neatly underneath itself (4). Keep going, gently forcing the sides of the dough down and underneath, to create a smooth, taut top and a rough underside. Avoid adding any extra flour during shaping if you possibly can.

The smooth, round cob is now ready to be transferred to a baking sheet for the proving stage.

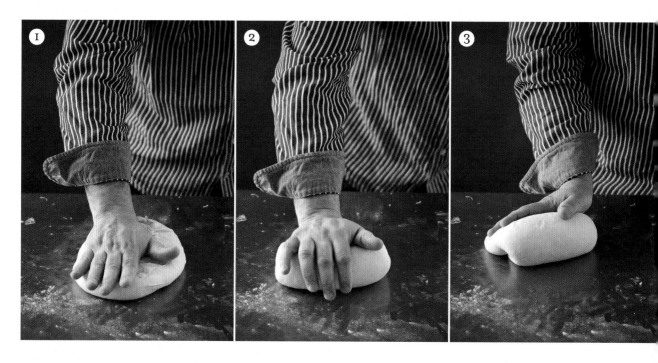

Oval 1

Oval

To shape an oval, tip out the risen dough onto a lightly floured surface and knock out the air. Flatten the dough into a rectangle, with the longer side facing you. Tuck each end in to the middle of the dough (1) so that they meet in the middle (2). Roll it up like a Swiss roll. The dough should now be smooth with a join line running along its length. Turn the dough so the line is pointing towards you and roll up again, but not as tight. Flatten out again, then roll up into a sausage. Roll, applying a little weight on either end to create slightly dropped sides (3). Pinch the ends to points (4) if required. When rolling the dough, use the full length of your hands from the tip of your fingers to the heel of your palm. The flattening and rolling knocks air out of the dough, helping to give an even crumb structure. Transfer the oval to a baking sheet for proving.

Bloomer

A bloomer is a long lozenge-shaped loaf, which looks particularly attractive when slashed before baking. To shape a bloomer, tip out the risen dough onto a lightly floured surface and knock out the air. Flatten the dough into a rectangle, with the longer side facing you. Tuck each end in towards the middle of the dough so that they meet in the middle, then roll up the dough like a Swiss roll (1) so you create a smooth top, with a join running along the length (2), which will become the base.

Roll it lightly, from your fingertips to the heel of your palms (3). If you apply too much pressure, you'll turn it into a square. It is now ready to be transferred to a baking sheet for proving.

Bloomer (1)   (2)   (3)

Plait

Plaited loaves look beautiful, and the plaiting technique increases the surface area of the loaf, so you get lots of lovely crust. When you shape these loaves, it is important to make sure that each strand of your plait is the same size and length (weigh them if you need to), and to press the ends of the strands together well to secure them when you start and finish plaiting.

To shape the most ambitious eight-strand plait (as for the variation on page 38), divide the dough into 8 pieces. Roll each out to a sausage ①, about 40cm in length – longer if you are feeling bold. Lay the long rolls out on a lightly floured surface and tack the gathered ends to the table with your thumb to form a sort of octopus ②.

You are now ready to follow the sequence. As they are laid out in front of you, number the lengths of dough 1–8. Remember that every time you move the strand the numbers will still be 1–8 in front of you.

First, take 8 under 7 and over 1 (you only do this once at the start). Then repeat the following moves until the plait is finished:

Take 8 over 5
Take 2 under 3 and over 8
Take 1 over 4
Take 7 under 6 and over 1

As you weave the strands, keep the plait as even as possible ③, so the strands are roughly the same length. When you have finished, secure the ends. You should have a pretty straight, even plait ④. It is now ready to be placed on a baking sheet for proving.

PROVING

This is the final rising stage of the shaped bread. As the bread proves, the yeast continues to feed and produce carbon dioxide, which causes the bread to rise again and gives it its characteristic aeration and structure. As the yeast ferments, it produces a cider-like smell that promises a great-tasting loaf. Typically cookery books advise you to leave the dough in a warm place, but bread will prove or rise in a fridge – it just takes longer.

The secret to making great bread is the time it takes to prove a loaf, and the longer the better. You can cover the dough with a plastic bag to stop it from forming a skin, but the bag needs to sit above the dough rather than touch it, otherwise it will restrict the expansion of the bread and hinder the proving process.

Generally, during the day, most homes are somewhere between 18°C and 24°C, which is more than adequate for proving bread. The days of putting your dough into an airing cupboard are over.

The best way to check whether your dough is ready for the oven is to gently press it and see if your fingers leave an indentation – the dough should spring back. This test is very good and with practice you'll learn to know precisely when is the optimum time to put breads in the oven.

ADDING STEAM

If I want a loaf to have a crisp, light crust and a slight sheen, I create a steamy oven environment. At the bakery, we have steam injectors in our ovens: water is pumped over hot pipes and steam floods into the oven for up to a minute at a time. To replicate this at home, when you turn the oven on, simply put a roasting tray on the bottom shelf to heat up. At the same time as you put your dough in to bake, pour enough hot water into the roasting tray from your kettle to two-thirds fill it. After 5–10 minutes – it's important not to open the oven door before 5 minutes – take a look at the tray. If most of the water has evaporated, top it up with some more. I don't bake all my bread with steam. If I want a rough, rustic, drier crust, I leave the oven dry.

CHECKING THE COLOUR OF YOUR BREAD

As a baker, one thing I never want to see is under-coloured, pale bread coming out of the oven. For flavour, texture and a good crust, you do need to get some colour on your loaf. You are looking for golden brown at the very least, ranging up to a deep, dark, toasty brown; white or yellowish bread is underdone. The picture opposite shows the range of colours you are aiming for to achieve well-baked bread.

BASIC BREAD TOOLS

The tools of my professional trade are many and varied, but you can use ordinary equipment in a domestic kitchen to very similar effect.

BAKING TRAYS AND BAKESTONES

Large, flat baking trays are a must; they should just fit the dimensions of your oven. You need heavy-duty trays that won't buckle in high heat. Some are completely flat, some have a raised lip along one edge; either will do. A heavy bakestone is a good investment if you intend to bake a lot of bread.

BREAD TINS

Bread tins come in a range of sizes. I usually use 1kg (2lb) tins with straight sides. You can buy these in any good kitchen shop, or online. The tins will need seasoning: rub with a bit of lard or margarine then put into your oven set at 200°C for 15 minutes. Turn off the oven and leave the tins to cool inside. This preparation will not only stop your loaves from sticking, but also help to form a good crust on your bread. Never wash your tins: you can scrape them and rub them with a rag drizzled with olive oil, but that's all.

SCOTCH SCRAPER

This plastic-handled scraper with its rigid, stainless steel blade is a crucial baking tool. Scotch scrapers are inexpensive and can be bought easily online. Use them for manipulating and cutting dough and for scraping down surfaces after kneading and shaping.

PEEL

This simple item of equipment allows you to transfer risen dough directly onto a heated bakestone or tray in the oven, which helps create a really good crust on the base of the bread. Dust the peel with fine semolina and put the risen dough on it, then shunt it onto the heated bakestone in the oven with a jerk of the wrist. Peels are now easy to buy online, though you can use a semolina-dusted baking tray to similar effect.

LINING PAPER

There are a variety of papers on the market but the ones to use are baking parchment or silicone paper, both of which are non-stick. Do not use greaseproof paper because it is liable to stick.

PLASTIC BAGS

Any large, clean plastic bags will be useful for covering the dough and creating a little aerated environment in which the dough can rise.

ELECTRIC MIXER

You'll see that, in some of my bread recipes, I suggest using a mixer with a dough hook to mix and knead the dough. I tend to specify this where the dough is very wet and sticky, or where a longer mixing time is required, but in fact, you could make any of the breads in the book using a mixer. It's an incredibly handy piece of equipment, which takes all the hard work out of kneading, and makes it quicker too.

OVENS

You can bake bread equally well in a gas or electric oven. An Aga or similar range cooker is also good for baking (it tends to produce a particularly good crust), but the baking times will need some adjustment – refer to the manufacturer's instructions for your particular cooker.

The important thing is to get to know your oven properly. It may well have a few hot-spots, and heat sources in ovens vary according to the model. No one knows your oven better than you do, so make it work for you. Whatever kind of oven you have, it pays to check its accuracy periodically: buy an oven thermometer and set your oven to 200°C/gas 6. When it has reached this temperature, pop your thermometer onto the middle shelf and take a measurement, then do the same for the bottom and top shelves. Check your readings and, if there is a discrepancy, get the manufacturer or an oven engineer to visit and reset your oven. I think anything more than 5 per cent out is unacceptable.

I've given temperatures in Centigrade for a non-fan oven. To convert for a fan oven, simply drop the temperature by 20°C. Gas ovens now vary in their conversions, newer ones having been brought in line with European conversions, so check the instructions for your particular model. You can usually find this information online if you no longer have the instruction booklet to hand. As a guide, here is the standard conversion from Centigrade to Gas:

170°C	Gas 3
180°C	Gas 4
190°C	Gas 5
200°C	Gas 6
210°C	Gas 6½
220°C	Gas 7

DOUGH THERMOMETER

Treat yourself to a dough thermometer. This is a probe that you can use to check the temperature of your ingredients and dough. Ideally, after mixing, your dough should be at 24–26°C, as this is the optimum range for yeast to work. Air temperature can affect this. In winter, for instance, you might need to use slightly warmer water when mixing your dough.

SOURDOUGH EQUIPMENT

A few additional items of equipment are useful for preparing sourdoughs, particularly to support these wetter doughs as they prove.

CLEAR PLASTIC CONTAINER

A 2-litre capacity, transparent container is perfect for raising a sourdough starter because it allows you to see how the yeast is behaving and how your dough is growing.

PROVING CLOTHS

I use a heavy cloth covered with flour as a proving surface for sourdoughs. Many of these doughs are very soft and slack and, if you put them on a smooth or shiny surface, such as baking parchment or silicone, they tend to 'flow' and spread sideways. A heavily floured cloth absorbs excess moisture from the dough as well as giving the dough something to 'grip', which helps it hold its shape and encourages it to rise upwards. You can buy traditional linen proving cloths, but these are not essential – any fairly thick, natural fibre cloth, such as a clean cotton tea towel, will do.

PROVING BASKETS

These help to give your sourdough loaves a beautiful shape, and of course you can use them for the basic breads in the following chapter too. They are also known as bannetons, and can be purchased in many shapes and sizes. The ones I use most often are a large oval, a large circle and large and small baguette shapes. Some come ready-lined with cloth, others you will need to line with a cloth yourself. In either case, they should be dusted well with flour before the dough goes in. Proving baskets can be bought online and are a great addition to any budding baker's tool kit. They can be used in most of my sourdough recipes, as an alternative to proving the dough on a cloth-lined tray (see above). You may find them useful, particularly if you are new to sourdoughs, because they hold the wet doughs in shape nicely.

Basic sourdough (see page 132) proving in a cloth-lined banneton (proving basket).

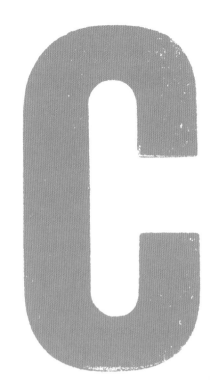

THIS CHAPTER is all about getting you started in the world of bread-making. It's really not difficult to bake your own bread. Like making a casserole, there's a bit to do at the beginning, then nature will take over and do most of the work for you. When you have some free time, gather your baking trays and ingredients together and start your journey. But be warned, bread-making is highly addictive. When you bring your first loaf out of the oven and taste it, there will be no going back: you will want to do this time and again.

Once you have tried a few of these basic breads, your confidence will grow enormously and you'll be keen to expand your repertoire and move on to the next chapter: Flavoured Breads.

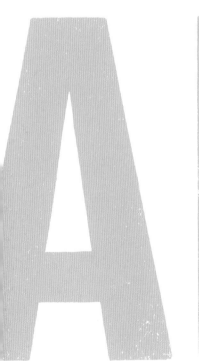

BASIC WHITE TIN BREAD

MAKES I large or 2 small loaves / PREP 3 hours / BAKE 30 minutes

You don't have to start your baking adventure with this simple white loaf, but you could do a lot worse. This recipe will introduce you to the key techniques you'll need for most bread-making. The dough is baked in a tin to give it that regular, easy-slicing shape that we are so fond of and it's ideal for sandwiches and toasting. Once you're confident baking this, you can try a simple white cob loaf (see page 38) using the same dough.

400g strong white bread flour, plus extra for dusting

8g salt

7g instant yeast

25g unsalted butter, softened

250ml cool water (see page 13)

Olive oil for kneading and oiling the tin

1. Tip the flour into a large mixing bowl and add the salt to one side of the bowl and the yeast to the other. Don't put the salt directly onto the yeast, as you may kill the yeast or at the very least slow it down.

2. Add the butter and three-quarters of the water, and turn the mixture round with your fingers. Continue to add the remaining water, a little at a time, until you've picked up all the flour from the sides of the bowl. You may not need to add all the water, or you may need to add a little more – you want dough that is soft, but not soggy. Use the mixture to clean the inside of the bowl and keep going until the mixture forms a rough dough.

3. Coat the work surface with a little oil; using olive oil rather than flour on the work surface to prevent sticking keeps the dough soft. Then tip the dough onto the surface and begin to knead (see page 16). Keep kneading for 5–10 minutes. Work through the initial wet stage until the dough starts to form a soft, smooth skin (see page 17).

4. When your dough feels smooth and silky, put it into a lightly oiled large bowl. Cover with a tea towel and leave to rise until at least doubled in size – this means at least 1 hour, but it's fine to leave it for 2 or even 3 hours. Resting the dough strengthens it and helps develop a robust crumb structure.

5. Prepare a 1kg loaf tin or two 500g loaf tins by rubbing olive oil over the inside. If you have not used the tin before, it should be seasoned (see page 28).

6. Tip your dough onto a lightly floured surface ①. If you are making 2 smaller loaves, divide the dough in half.

7. First shape into a ball by folding the dough inwards repeatedly ② until all the air is knocked out and the dough is smooth. Then form into an oblong by flattening the dough out slightly and folding the sides into the middle. Roll the whole lot up – the top should be smooth with a join running along the length of the base ③. Put your dough into the prepared tin ④, making sure the join is underneath.

(continued overleaf)

8. Put the tin(s) inside clean plastic bag(s) and leave it to prove for about 1 hour, until the dough is at least doubled in size and springs back quickly if you prod it lightly with your finger. Meanwhile, heat your oven to 220°C and put a roasting tray in the bottom to heat up.

9. Dust the risen, springy dough with flour and slash the top with a knife — a sharp serrated blade is ideal. Fill the roasting tray in the oven with hot water to create steam and put the bread into the oven.

10. Bake for 30 minutes or until the bread is cooked through. Check by tipping the loaf out of the tin and tapping the base — it should sound hollow. Cool the loaf, out of the tin, on a wire rack.

WHOLEMEAL TIN BREAD

Follow the recipe above, but use 350g strong wholemeal bread flour and 50g strong white bread flour. You will need a little more water too, as wholemeal flour absorbs more — about 265ml. (Wholemeal tin loaves are shown in this photograph.)

WHITE COB LOAF

MAKES 1 loaf / PREP 3 hours / BAKE 30 minutes

This recipe uses the same dough as the basic tin bread (see page 34) but in a slightly bigger quantity and the loaf is shaped by hand, rather than in a tin.

500g strong white bread flour, plus extra for dusting

10g salt

10g instant yeast

30g unsalted butter, softened

320ml cool water

Olive oil for kneading

1. Tip the flour into a large mixing bowl. Add the salt to one side of the bowl and the yeast to the other. Add the butter and three-quarters of the water, and turn the mixture round with your fingers. Continue to add the remaining water, a little at a time, until you've picked up all the flour from the sides of the bowl. You may not need to add all the water, or you may need to add a little more – you want dough that is soft, but not soggy. Use the mixture to clean the inside of the bowl and keep going until the mixture forms a rough dough.

2. Coat the work surface with a little olive oil, then tip the dough onto it and begin to knead. Keep kneading for 5–10 minutes. Work through the initial wet stage until the dough starts to form a soft, smooth skin. When your dough feels smooth and silky, put it into a lightly oiled large bowl. Cover with a tea towel and leave to rise until at least doubled in size – at least 1 hour, but it's fine to leave it for 2 or even 3 hours.

3. Line a baking tray with baking parchment or silicone paper.

4. Once risen, the dough should be bouncy and shiny. Scrape it out of the bowl onto a lightly floured surface. First shape into a ball by folding it inwards repeatedly until all the air is knocked out and the dough is smooth. Then form it into a round, smooth cob shape (see pages 20–1).

5. Put the dough on the baking tray and place in a clean plastic bag. Leave to prove for about 1 hour, until the dough is at least doubled in size and springs back quickly if you prod it lightly with your finger. Meanwhile, heat your oven to 230°C and put a roasting tray in the bottom to heat up.

6. Dust the dough with some flour, then slash deeply with a knife. Fill the hot roasting tray in the oven with hot water: this will create steam and give your bread a lighter crust. Put your bread into the oven and bake for 30 minutes or until it is cooked through and sounds hollow when tapped on the base. Cool on a wire rack.

EIGHT-STRAND PLAIT

Follow the above recipe, but use 600g flour, 12g each of yeast and salt, 35g butter and about 400ml water to make your dough. Once risen and knocked back, divide the dough into 8 equal pieces and plait, following the instructions on page 24. Put the shaped dough onto a baking tray lined with silicone paper or baking parchment. Put the tray inside a clean plastic bag and leave to prove for about 1 hour, until the dough is doubled in size and springs back quickly if you prod it with your finger. Bake as above.

WHOLEMEAL LOAF

MAKES I loaf / PREP 3 hours / BAKE 30 minutes

This simple wholemeal loaf includes a little white flour for lightness but is still full of nutty, wholegrain flavour. You could always increase the proportion of white flour for a more delicate texture, or use all wholemeal flour if you are a purist. This bread makes excellent toast — very good with pâtés and smoked fish.

400g stoneground strong wholemeal bread flour, plus extra for dusting

100g strong white bread flour

10g salt

10g instant yeast

40g unsalted butter, softened

320ml tepid water

Olive oil for kneading

1. Tip the flours into a large mixing bowl and add the salt to one side of the bowl and the yeast to the other. Add the butter and three-quarters of the water, and turn the mixture round with your fingers. Continue to add water a little at a time until you've picked up all the flour from the sides of the bowl. You may not need to add all the water, or you may need to add a little more — you want dough that is soft, but not soggy. Use the mixture to clean the inside of the bowl, folding the edges into the middle. Keep going until the mixture forms a rough dough.

2. Coat the work surface with a little olive oil, then tip the dough onto it and begin to knead. Keep kneading for 5–10 minutes. Work through the initial wet stage until the dough starts to form a soft, smooth skin.

3. When your dough feels smooth and silky, put it into a lightly oiled large bowl. Cover with a tea towel and leave to rise until at least doubled in size — at least I hour, but it's fine to leave it for 2 or even 3 hours.

4. Line a baking tray with baking parchment or silicone paper.

5. Dust your work surface lightly with flour and tip your dough onto it. Knock the air out of the dough by folding it inwards repeatedly until the dough is smooth. Flatten the dough and roll it up into a sausage, then roll this out with your hands until it is about 30cm long. Tie the dough in a knot and place on the prepared baking tray.

6. Put the tray into a clean plastic bag. Leave to prove for about I hour, until the dough is at least doubled in size and springs back quickly if you prod it lightly with your finger. Meanwhile, heat your oven to 220°C and put a roasting tray in the bottom to heat up.

7. Gently rub flour all over the proved dough. Put the loaf into the oven and fill the roasting tray with hot water. This will create steam in the oven, which helps give the bread a lighter crust. Bake the loaf for 30 minutes, then check it is cooked by tapping the base — it should sound hollow. Cool on a wire rack.

SODA BREAD

MAKES 1 loaf / PREP 20 minutes / BAKE 30 minutes

Leavened with bicarbonate of soda rather than yeast, soda bread is really quick to make. It's perfect when you want to knock up something fast for lunch or supper. The recipe is very adaptable: you can add grated Cheddar and chopped raw onion or chopped pitted olives and sun-dried tomatoes to the mix for a flavoured bread. You can also use half wholemeal flour to white flour.

500g plain white flour, plus extra for dusting

1 tsp bicarbonate of soda

1 tsp salt

400ml buttermilk

1. Heat your oven to 200°C and line a baking tray with baking parchment or silicone paper.

2. Put all the dry ingredients into a large bowl and mix well, then stir in the buttermilk to form a sticky dough. Tip the dough onto a lightly floured surface and shape it quickly into a ball. Flatten the ball a little with your hand.

3. Put the dough on the baking tray. Mark it into quarters, cutting deeply through the bread, almost but not quite through to the base. Dust with a little flour.

4. Bake for 30 minutes or until the loaf is cooked through — it should be golden brown and sound hollow when tapped on the base. Leave it to cool on a wire rack. Soda bread is best eaten within a day of baking. It freezes well.

WRAPS

MAKES 15–17 / PREP 1–2 hours / FRY 3 minutes per wrap

These lovely, simple flatbreads are soft and tender enough to wrap and fold, so you can fill them with all sorts of tasty ingredients. You can serve them unfilled too, just as they come, to dip into a soup or scoop up a chilli, for example. I like to keep some in the freezer because they defrost very quickly, making them ideal for quick meals.

500g strong white bread flour, plus extra for dusting

10g salt

30g caster sugar

10g instant yeast

30g unsalted butter, softened

320ml cool water

A little vegetable oil for cooking

1. Tip the flour into a large mixing bowl and add the salt and sugar to one side of the bowl and the yeast to the other. Add the butter and three-quarters of the water, and turn the mixture round with your fingers. Continue to add water a little at a time until you've picked up all the flour from the sides of the bowl. You may not need to add all the water, or you may need to add a little more – you want dough that is soft, but not soggy. Use the mixture to clean the inside of the bowl, folding the edges into the middle. Keep going until the mixture forms a rough dough.

2. Tip the dough onto a lightly floured surface and knead well for 5–10 minutes. Do not add too much flour to your work surface as this will make the dough too dry.

3. When your dough feels smooth and silky, put it into a lightly oiled large bowl. Cover with a tea towel and leave to rise until at least doubled in size – at least 1 hour, but it's fine to leave it for 2 or even 3 hours.

4. Dust a work surface lightly with flour and tip your dough onto it. Fold it inwards repeatedly until all the air is knocked out and the dough is smooth. Divide into 60g pieces.

5. You may find it easier to shape and cook your wraps in batches. Roll each piece into a ball. Using a rolling pin, roll out each ball to a circle, 20cm in diameter, rolling out from the middle up, then from the middle down, and turning the dough regularly to prevent it from sticking to the work surface.

6. Heat a 23–25cm frying pan over a high heat and add 1 tbsp vegetable oil. When it starts to smoke, place one of the dough rounds in the pan and fry for 2 minutes. Flip the bread over and cook the other side for 1 minute. Repeat to cook the rest of the dough rounds, adding a little more oil to the pan if you need to. When each one is cooked, place it on top of the last. Stacking the wraps like this traps steam between them and helps to soften them as they cool.

7. Once cool, wrap the breads in cling film. Use within 24 hours, or freeze them interleaved with cling film or baking parchment to keep them separate, otherwise they will freeze into a solid mass.

PITTA BREADS

MAKES 6–8 / PREP 1–2 hours / BAKE 5–10 minutes per batch

You'll be amazed how easy it is to make authentic-looking pitta breads at home. These are delicious when freshly baked, split open and stuffed with good things such as hummus, salad and falafel – or almost anything else that takes your fancy. They also freeze well and you can pop them straight from the freezer into the toaster.

250g strong white
   bread flour

5g salt

7g instant yeast

160ml cool water

2 tsp olive oil, plus
   extra for kneading

Fine semolina
   (or extra flour)
   for dusting

1. Tip the flour into a large mixing bowl and add the salt to one side of the bowl and the yeast to the other. Add three-quarters of the water and the olive oil, and turn the mixture round with your fingers. Continue to add the remaining water, a little at a time, until you've picked up all the flour from the sides of the bowl. You may not need to add all the water, or you may need to add a little more – you want dough that is soft, but not soggy. Use the mixture to clean the inside of the bowl and keep going until the mixture forms a rough dough.

2. Coat the work surface with a little olive oil, then tip the dough onto it and begin to knead. Keep kneading for 5–10 minutes. Work through the initial wet stage until the dough starts to form a soft, smooth skin.

3. When your dough feels smooth and silky, put it into a lightly oiled large bowl. Cover with a tea towel and leave to rise until at least doubled in size – at least 1 hour, but it's fine to leave it for 2 or even 3 hours. Meanwhile, heat your oven to 220°C and put a bakestone or baking tray in the centre to heat up.

4. Dust a work surface lightly with fine semolina or flour. Tip your risen dough onto it. Fold it inwards repeatedly until all the air is knocked out and the dough is smooth. Divide the dough into 6–8 equal pieces and shape each piece into a ball, keeping them covered with a tea towel as you work. With a rolling pin, start rolling out the pieces of dough into rough oval shapes, about 3mm thick, stopping when you have as many as will fit on the stone or baking tray with some space in between.

5. Take the hot stone or tray from the oven, scatter with a little semolina, then lay the pitta breads on it. Bake for 5–10 minutes, taking the pittas out of the oven as soon as you start to see any colour on them. Repeat with the remaining dough. Leave the pittas to cool, keeping them covered with a cloth as they do so; the trapped steam will keep them soft. Eat within 24 hours or freeze.

CHAPATIS

MAKES 6 / PREP I hour / FRY 3–4 minutes per chapati

Traditionally, these Indian flatbreads are baked over an open flame, simply held in the hand. You have to be very quick, turning and moving the dough above the flame without letting it – or your hands – burn. It helps to have asbestos hands! Indian girls are taught how to do this from a young age and this skill is taken to be the sign of a good cook. Thankfully, chapatis are also very good cooked in a hot frying pan. These are delicious for scooping up almost any curry.

250g strong wholemeal bread flour, plus extra for dusting

5g salt

20ml olive oil, plus extra for cooking

160ml water

1. Mix all the ingredients together in a bowl to form a rough dough. Tip out onto a lightly floured surface and knead for 5–10 minutes until the dough is elastic and smooth. Put the dough into an oiled bowl, cover and leave to rest for 30 minutes.

2. Divide the dough into 6 equal pieces. Roll each one into a ball, then into a thin disc, about 20cm in diameter.

3. Heat a frying pan over a medium-high heat and brush with a tiny bit of olive oil. When the pan is nice and hot, cook the chapatis, one at a time, for 1½–2 minutes on each side until browned. Serve straight away.

BARM CAKES

MAKES 12–13 / PREP 3½ hours / BAKE 10 minutes

These soft rolls take their name from the yeasty froth or 'barm' that collects
on the surface of fermenting beer, which was once used to leaven them.
They originated in the Northwest and were sold in all the local bakeries
around the Wirral where I grew up. In other parts of the country, you will
come across similar rolls under various different names: baps, batch rolls,
flour rolls, soft rolls etc.

500g strong white
   bread flour, plus
   extra for dusting

10g salt

40g caster sugar

10g instant yeast

40g unsalted butter,
   softened

320ml cool water

1. Put the flour into a large bowl. Add the salt and sugar to one side and
   the yeast to the other. Add the butter and three-quarters of the water,
   and turn the mixture round with your fingers. Continue to add water
   a little at a time until you've picked up all the flour from the sides of the
   bowl. You may not need to add all the water, or you may need to add a
   little more – you want dough that is soft, but not soggy. Use the mixture
   to clean the inside of the bowl, folding the edges into the middle. Keep
   going until the mixture forms a rough dough.

2. Tip the dough onto a lightly floured surface. Knead for 5–10 minutes,
   working through the initial wet stage until the dough starts to form a
   soft, smooth skin.

3. When your dough feels smooth and silky, put it into a lightly oiled large
   bowl. Cover with a tea towel and leave to rise until at least doubled in
   size – at least 1 hour, but it's fine to leave it for 2 or even 3 hours.

4. Once the dough is risen, tip it out onto a lightly floured surface. Fold
   it inwards repeatedly until all the air is knocked out and the dough is
   smooth. Divide the dough into 12 or 13 pieces, each weighing about 70g.
   Roll each one into a smooth ball by placing it into a cage formed by your
   hand and the table and moving your hand around in a circular motion,
   rotating the ball rapidly. The shape will come with practice.

5. Put the rolls back onto a heavily floured surface and leave to rest for
   30 minutes. Meanwhile, prepare your baking trays – you will need at
   least three – by lining them with baking parchment or silicone paper.

6. Once rested, roll out the dough balls, using a floured rolling pin, until
   they are twice their original diameter. Lift onto the prepared baking
   trays, spacing them apart to allow room for spreading, and sprinkle with
   flour. Put each tray inside a clean plastic bag and leave to prove for about
   1 hour, until the dough is doubled in size and springs back quickly if you
   prod it lightly with your finger. Meanwhile, heat your oven to 210°C.

7. When the barm cakes are very light and airy, bake them for 10 minutes
   only, then leave them to cool on the baking trays. Once cooled, store in
   a lidded container, to keep them soft.

COTTAGE LOAF

MAKES 1 loaf / PREP 3 hours / BAKE 30 minutes

This British classic is one of the original 'oven bottoms' — a loaf left on the floor of the oven to produce a heavier, tastier crust. You can replicate this by baking your loaf on a preheated bakestone.

**500g strong white
bread flour, plus
extra for dusting**

10g salt

10g instant yeast

**30g unsalted butter,
softened**

330ml cool water

Olive oil for kneading

1. Tip the flour into a large mixing bowl and add the salt to one side of the bowl and the yeast to the other. Add the butter and three-quarters of the water, stirring continuously with your hand. Continue to add water a little at a time, until you've picked up all the flour from the sides of the bowl. You may not need to add all the water, or you may need to add a little more — you want dough that is soft, but not soggy. Use the mixture to clean the inside of the bowl and keep going until the mixture forms a rough dough.

2. Coat a work surface with a little olive oil. Tip the dough onto it and knead for 5–10 minutes, working through the initial wet stage until the dough feels smooth and silky. Put it into a lightly oiled large bowl. Cover with a tea towel and leave to rise until at least doubled in size — at least 1 hour, but it's fine to leave it for 2 or even 3 hours.

3. Tip the dough onto a lightly floured surface. Fold it inwards repeatedly until all the air is knocked out and the dough is smooth. Divide it into 2 pieces, one twice as big as the other. Shape the larger piece into a ball by folding the dough over and tucking the sides underneath (as for a cob, see pages 20–1). Do this at least 3 times and the dough will become a lot tighter and more stable. Shape the smaller piece in the same way.

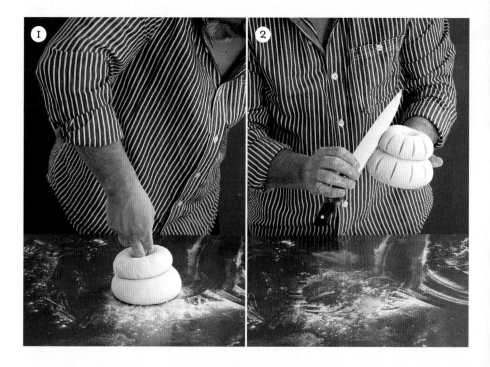

4. Place the smaller piece on top of the larger ball. Dust your middle finger and forefinger with flour and push them right down through both balls of dough ⓘ. Repeat this twice. Lift up your loaf and carefully make vertical cuts with a very sharp knife from the top to the bottom ②.

5. Place the loaf on a baking tray lined with baking parchment and put into a clean plastic bag. Leave to prove for about 1 hour, until the dough is at least doubled in size and springs back quickly if you prod it lightly with a finger. Heat your oven to 210°C and put a roasting tray in the bottom.

6. Fill the roasting tray with hot water and put the loaf into the oven. Bake for 30 minutes, until it sounds hollow when tapped. Cool on a wire rack.

CRUSTY DINNER ROLLS

MAKES 12 / PREP 3 hours / BAKE 15–20 minutes

These have a gorgeous, golden crust and a lovely tender crumb
– perfect for tearing open and smearing with butter.

**500g strong white
bread flour, plus
extra for dusting**

10g salt

10g instant yeast

**20g unsalted butter,
softened**

320ml cool water

1. Put the flour, salt and yeast into the bowl of a mixer fitted with a dough hook (don't put the salt directly on top of the yeast). Add the butter and three-quarters of the water and begin mixing on a slow speed. As the dough starts to come together, slowly add the remaining water. When all the water has been added, mix for a further 5 minutes on a medium speed. The dough should now be soft and elastic.

2. Tip the dough into a lightly oiled bowl, cover with a tea towel and leave until at least doubled in size – at least 1 hour, but it's fine to leave it for 2 or even 3 hours.

3. Line 2 baking trays with baking parchment or silicone paper.

4. Scrape the dough out of the bowl onto a lightly floured surface. Fold it inwards repeatedly until all the air is knocked out and the dough is smooth. Divide into 12 pieces. Roll each one into a ball by placing it into a cage formed by your hand and the table, and moving your hand around in a circular motion, rotating the ball rapidly. The shape will come with practice. Put the balls onto the prepared baking trays, spacing them slightly apart.

5. Place each tray in a clean plastic bag. Leave to prove for about 1 hour, until the dough is at least doubled in size and springs back quickly if you prod it lightly with your finger. Meanwhile, heat your oven to 220°C and put a roasting tray in the bottom to heat up.

6. Once proved, sprinkle the rolls with a little flour and cut a cross in the top of each one with a sharp knife or scissors. Fill the roasting tray with hot water, then put your rolls into the oven. Bake for 15–20 minutes, until they are golden in colour and sound hollow when tapped on the base. Cool on a wire rack.

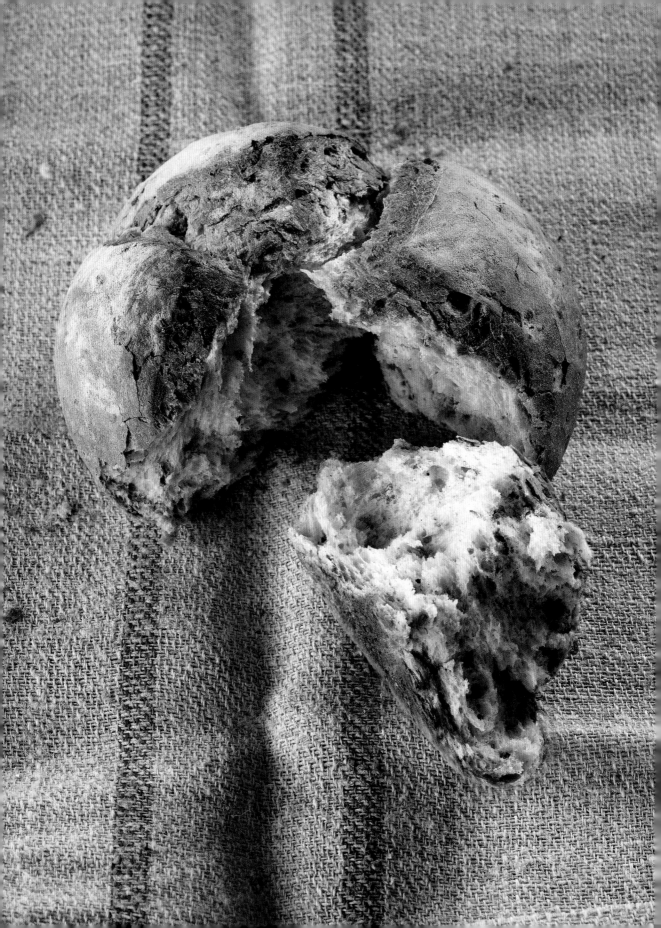

MALTED LOAF

MAKES I loaf / PREP 3 hours / BAKE 30 minutes

Malted flours are white rather than wholemeal, but enhanced with malted
grains of wheat, which give the finished bread a lovely flavour and texture.
I particularly like malted bread with cheese and chutney or pickle.

**500g malted bread
    flour**

10g salt

10g instant yeast

**30g unsalted butter,
    softened**

300ml cool water

Olive oil for kneading

**Wholemeal bread flour
    for dusting**

1. Tip the flour into a large mixing bowl and add the salt to one side of
   the bowl and the yeast to the other. Add the butter and three-quarters
   of the water, and turn the mixture round with your fingers. Continue to
   add the remaining water, a little at a time, until you've picked up all the
   flour from the sides of the bowl. You may not need to add all the water,
   or you may need to add a little more – you want dough that is soft, but
   not soggy. Use the mixture to clean the inside of the bowl and keep
   going until the mixture forms a rough dough.

2. Coat the work surface with a little olive oil, then tip the dough onto
   it and start to knead. Keep kneading for at least 10 minutes. Work
   through the initial wet stage until the dough starts to form a soft,
   smooth skin.

3. When your dough feels smooth and silky, put it into a lightly oiled large
   bowl. Cover with a tea towel and leave to rise until at least doubled in
   size – at least 1 hour, but it's fine to leave it for 2 or even 3 hours.

4. Line a baking tray with baking parchment or silicone paper.

5. Scrape the dough out of the bowl onto a lightly floured surface. Fold
   it inwards repeatedly until all the air is knocked out and the dough is
   smooth. Form it into a round, smooth cob shape (see pages 20–1) and
   place on the prepared baking tray.

6. Put the tray inside a clean plastic bag. Leave to prove for about 1 hour,
   until the dough is at least doubled in size and springs back quickly if you
   prod it lightly with your finger. Heat your oven to 220°C.

7. Dust the top of the loaf with flour and cut a deep cross on the top. Bake
   for 30 minutes or until the bread sounds hollow when you tap it on the
   base. Cool on a wire rack.

SPELT BREAD

MAKES I loaf / PREP 3 hours / BAKE 30 minutes

I always bake spelt dough in a tin, to counteract its tendency to spread outwards. The result is a well-flavoured, easy-slicing loaf. Spelt bread is excellent toasted and slathered with butter and marmalade for breakfast.

500g spelt flour, plus
    extra for dusting
10g salt
10g instant yeast
30g unsalted butter,
    softened
300ml tepid water
Olive oil for kneading
    and oiling the tin

1. Tip the flour into a large mixing bowl and add the salt to one side of the bowl and the yeast to the other. Add the butter and three-quarters of the water, and turn the mixture round with your fingers. Continue to add the water, a little at a time, until you've picked up all the flour from the sides of the bowl. You may not need to add all the water, or you may need to add a little more — you want dough that is soft, but not soggy. Use the mixture to clean the inside of the bowl and keep going until the mixture forms a rough dough.

2. Spelt flour is different from conventional flours in that it has slightly less gluten and therefore the dough takes longer to knead properly. Coat the work surface with a little olive oil, then tip the dough onto it and begin to knead. Keep kneading for at least 10 minutes.

3. When your dough feels smooth and silky, put it into a lightly oiled large bowl. Cover with a tea towel and leave to rise until at least doubled in size — at least 1 hour, but it's fine to leave it for 2 or even 3 hours.

4. Brush a 1kg loaf tin with a little olive oil (or you can use melted butter).

5. When the dough is rested, tip it out onto a lightly floured surface. Fold it inwards repeatedly until all the air is knocked out and the dough is smooth. Form the dough into an oblong by flattening it out slightly and folding the sides into the middle. Roll the whole lot up — the top should be smooth with a join running along the length of the base. Put your dough into the prepared tin, making sure the join is underneath.

6. Put the tin inside a clean plastic bag and leave to prove for about 1 hour, until the dough is at least doubled in size and springs back quickly if you prod it lightly with your finger. Meanwhile, heat your oven to 220°C and put a roasting tray in the bottom to heat up.

7. Once the dough is proved, dust the top with a little flour and cut several diagonal slashes across the top. Fill the roasting tray with hot water to create steam and put the bread into the oven. Bake for 30 minutes or until cooked through. Check by tipping the loaf out of the tin and tapping the base to see if it sounds hollow. Leave to cool, out of the tin, on a wire rack.

MILK LOAF

MAKES 1 loaf / PREP 3 hours / BAKE 25 minutes

A traditional ingredient in bread-making for centuries, milk creates a loaf
with a soft, light texture and a delicately sweet flavour. You may prefer to
bake it as a cob (see page 20), bloomer (see page 23) or plait (see below).

**500g strong white
bread flour, plus
extra for dusting**

10g salt

25g caster sugar

10g instant yeast

**30g unsalted butter,
softened**

**320ml warm full-fat
milk**

Olive oil for kneading

1. Tip the flour into a large mixing bowl and add the salt and sugar to one
   side of the bowl and the yeast to the other. Add the butter and three-
   quarters of the milk. At this stage, move the flour around gently with
   your fingertips. Continue to add the remaining milk, a little at a time,
   until you've picked up all of the flour from the sides of the bowl. You
   may not need to add all the milk, or you may need to add a little more
   — you want dough that is soft, but not soggy. Use the mixture to clean
   the inside of the bowl and keep going until it forms a soft dough.

2. Coat the work surface with a little olive oil, then tip the dough onto it
   and start to knead. Keep kneading for 5–10 minutes. Work through the
   initial wet stage until the dough starts to form a soft, smooth skin. When
   your dough feels smooth and silky, put it into a lightly oiled large bowl.
   Cover with a tea towel and leave to rise until at least doubled in size — at
   least 1 hour, but it's fine to leave it for 2 or even 3 hours.

3. Brush a 1kg loaf tin with a little olive oil (or you can use melted butter).

4. Tip your dough onto a lightly floured surface. Fold it inwards repeatedly
   until all the air is knocked out and the dough is smooth. Then form it
   into an oblong by flattening the dough out slightly and folding the sides
   into the middle. Roll the whole lot up — the top should be smooth with
   a join running along the length of the base. Put into the prepared tin,
   making sure the join is underneath. Dust the top lightly with flour and
   slash lengthways.

5. Put the tin inside a clean plastic bag and leave to prove for about 1 hour,
   until the dough is at least doubled in size and springs back quickly if you
   prod it lightly with your finger. Meanwhile, heat your oven to 210°C.

6. Bake for 25 minutes or until the bread sounds hollow when tapped on
   the base. Leave to cool, out of the tin, on a wire rack.

THREE-STRAND PLAIT

Divide the knocked-back dough into 3 equal pieces and roll each into
a sausage, at least 25cm long. Join them together at one end, ready for
plaiting. Start with the outer piece on the right and lift it over the middle
piece, then lift the piece on the left over the middle, then the right over the
middle and left over the middle. Repeat this sequence until you reach the
end. Tuck the ends underneath. Lift the plait onto a baking tray lined with
silicone paper or baking parchment. Prove and bake as above.

ALE BREAD ROLLS

MAKES 14 / PREP 3 hours / BAKE 30 minutes

A good-quality beer is essential for this recipe. I usually go for Kentish Spitfire ale but any good, flavoursome ale will work. I like to think that the flavours in this hearty bread are similar to those that medieval bakers would have created.

400g strong white bread flour, plus extra for dusting

100g strong wholemeal bread flour

10g salt

10g instant yeast

30g unsalted butter, softened

300ml good-quality ale, such as Spitfire

Olive oil for kneading

1. Tip the flours into a large mixing bowl, and add the salt to one side of the bowl and the yeast to the other. Add the butter and three-quarters of the ale. At this stage, just move the flour around gently with your fingertips. Continue to add the ale, a little at a time, until you've picked up all the flour from the sides of the bowl. You may not need to add all the ale, or you may need to add a little more (or add a splash of water) — you want dough that is soft, but not soggy. Use the mixture to clean the inside of the bowl and keep going until the mixture forms a rough dough.

2. Coat the work surface with a little olive oil, then tip the dough onto it and begin to knead. Keep kneading for 5–10 minutes. Work through the initial wet stage until the dough starts to form a soft, smooth skin.

3. When your dough feels smooth and silky, put it into a lightly oiled large bowl. Cover with a tea towel and leave to rise until at least doubled in size — at least 1 hour, but it's fine to leave it for 2 or even 3 hours.

4. Line 2 baking trays with baking parchment or silicone paper.

5. Tip the dough onto a lightly floured surface. Fold it inwards repeatedly until all the air is knocked out and the dough is smooth. Divide into 14 equal pieces, each weighing about 60g. Roll each one into a ball by placing it in a cage formed by your hand and the table, and moving your hand around in a circular motion, rotating the ball rapidly. The shape will come with practice. Place one dough ball in the middle of each prepared baking tray and position the rest of the balls around, so they are almost touching and you have 7 balls on each tray.

6. Put each tray into a clean plastic bag and leave to prove for about 1 hour, until the dough is at least doubled in size and springs back quickly if you prod it lightly with your finger. Meanwhile, heat your oven to 210°C.

7. Dust the rolls with flour and give each one 3 little snips with scissors (leave the ones in the middle uncut if you like). Bake for 30 minutes, until the rolls are golden in colour and sound hollow when tapped on the base. Leave to cool on a wire rack. Eat with lots of butter.

BAGUETTES

MAKES 4 or 5 / PREP 3 hours / BAKE 25 minutes

This light, airy baguette has a wonderful crisp golden crust. To get the right result, you need a relatively wet dough, which is why I recommend using a mixer. Most home ovens can't fit the length of a traditional baguette, so smaller ones are the order of the day.

500g strong white
   bread flour, plus
   extra for dusting
10g salt
10g instant yeast
370ml cool water
Olive oil for kneading

1. Lightly oil a 2–3 litre square plastic container. (It's important to use a square tub as it helps shape the dough.)

2. Put the flour, salt and yeast into the bowl of a mixer fitted with a dough hook (don't put the salt directly on top of the yeast). Add three-quarters of the water and begin mixing on a slow speed. As the dough starts to come together, slowly add the remaining water, then continue to mix on a medium speed for 5–7 minutes, until you have a glossy, elastic dough.

3. Tip the dough into the prepared tub. Cover with a tea towel and leave until at least doubled in size – about 1 hour.

4. Line 2 baking trays with baking parchment or silicone paper.

5. Coat the work surface with a little olive oil, then carefully tip the dough onto it. Rather than knocking it back, handle it gently so you keep as much air in the dough as possible. This helps to create the irregular, airy texture of a really good baguette. The dough will be wet to the touch but still lively.

6. Divide the dough into 4 or 5 pieces. Shape each piece into an oblong by flattening the dough out slightly and folding the sides into the middle. Then roll each up into a sausage – the top should be smooth with a join running along the length of the base. Now, beginning in the middle, roll out each sausage with your hands. Don't force it out by pressing heavily. Concentrate on the backwards and forwards movement and gently use the weight of your arms to roll out the dough to the length of your oven trays.

7. Place 2 or 3 baguettes on each baking tray. Put each tray inside a clean plastic bag and leave to prove for about 1 hour, until the dough is at least doubled in size and springs back quickly if you prod it lightly with your finger. Meanwhile, heat your oven to 220°C and put a roasting tray in the bottom to heat up.

8. When your baguettes are risen and light, dust them lightly with flour. Then slash each one 3 times along its length on the diagonal, using a razor blade or very sharp knife. Fill the roasting tray with hot water to create steam and put the bread into the oven. Bake for 25 minutes, or until the baguettes are golden brown and have a slight sheen. Cool on a wire rack.

CIABATTA

MAKES 4 / PREP 2 hours / BAKE 25 minutes

This straightforward ciabatta recipe is relatively easy and satisfying to make.
To get that classic ciabatta shape and open texture, you need a very wet and
sloppy dough, so you really have to make it in an electric mixer. Serve this
thin-crusted, light-textured bread warm for breakfast, with soups or salads,
or split, toasted and filled with salami, prosciutto or cheese for an Italian-
style sandwich.

**500g strong white
bread flour, plus
extra for dusting**

10g salt

10g instant yeast

40ml olive oil

400ml tepid water

**Fine semolina for
dusting (optional)**

1. Lightly oil a 2–3 litre square plastic container. (It's important to use
   a square tub as it helps shape the dough.)

2. Put the flour, salt and yeast into the bowl of a mixer fitted with a dough
   hook (don't put the salt directly on top of the yeast). Add the olive oil
   and three-quarters of the water and begin mixing on a slow speed.
   As the dough starts to come together, slowly add the remaining water.
   Then mix for a further 5–8 minutes on a medium speed until the
   dough is smooth and stretchy.

3. Tip the dough into the prepared tub, cover with a tea towel and leave
   until at least doubled, even trebled in size – 1–2 hours or longer.

4. Heat your oven to 220°C and line 2 baking trays with baking parchment
   or silicone paper.

5. Dust your work surface heavily with flour – add some semolina too,
   if you have some. Carefully tip out the dough (it will be very wet) onto
   the work surface, trying to retain a rough square shape. Rather than
   knocking it back, handle it gently so you keep as much air in the dough
   as possible. Coat the top of the dough with more flour and/or semolina.
   Cut the dough in half lengthways and divide each half lengthways into
   2 strips. You should now have 4 pieces of dough. Stretch each piece of
   dough lengthways a little and place on the prepared baking trays.

6. Leave the ciabatta dough to rest for a further 10 minutes, then bake
   for 25 minutes, or until the loaves are golden brown and sound hollow
   when tapped on the base. Cool on a wire rack.

FOCACCIA

MAKES 2 / PREP 3 hours / BAKE 15 minutes

This lovely, oil-rich Italian bread is great for sharing and is particularly good served still warm with extra virgin olive oil for dipping, and perhaps some salad and olives or antipasti. The dough here is really quite wet, so you might well prefer to knead it in a mixer. However, I've suggested you make it by hand because it's useful to get to know the feel of a good, wet dough and this one is a little more manageable than, for example, a ciabatta.

500g strong white
    bread flour, plus
    extra for dusting
10g salt
10g instant yeast
140ml olive oil, plus
    extra for kneading
    and to finish
360ml cool water
Fine semolina for
    dusting (optional)

To finish
Flaky sea salt
Dried oregano

1. Lightly oil a 2–3 litre square plastic container. (It's important to use a square tub as it helps shape the dough.)

2. Tip the flour into a large mixing bowl and add the salt to one side of the bowl and the yeast to the other. Add 40ml of the olive oil and three-quarters of the water, and turn the mixture round with your fingers. Continue to add water, a little at a time, until you've picked up all the flour from the sides of the bowl. You may not need to add all the water, or you may need to add a little more. You want dough that is very soft — wetter than a standard bread dough. Use the mixture to clean the inside of the bowl and keep going until the mixture forms a rough dough.

3. Coat the work surface with some of the remaining olive oil, then tip the dough onto it and begin to knead. Keep kneading for 5–10 minutes. Work through the initial wet stage until the dough starts to form a soft, smooth skin. This is supposed to be a wet, sticky dough, so try not to add more flour.

4. When your dough feels soft and elastic, put the dough into the oiled tub. Cover with a tea towel and leave to rise until at least doubled in size — about 1 hour.

5. Line 2 baking trays with baking parchment and drizzle with olive oil.

6. Put more olive oil on the work surface and dust with fine semolina if you have some. Carefully tip the dough onto the surface. Rather than knocking it back, handle it gently so you keep as much air in the dough as possible. Divide the dough in half. Stretch each piece out to a flat, even piece and place on a baking tray.

7. Put each tray into a clean plastic bag and leave to prove for about 1 hour, until the dough is doubled in size and springs back quickly if you prod it lightly with your finger. Meanwhile, heat your oven to 220°C.

8. Make deep dimples in the focaccia with your fingers, pushing them all the way through the dough to the bottom. Drizzle each focaccia with olive oil and sprinkle with a little flaky sea salt and oregano, then bake for 15 minutes, or until cooked through. Tap the bottom of the focaccia and you should hear a hollow sound. Trickle with more olive oil, then cool on a wire rack.

FOUGASSE

MAKES 1 / PREP 2 hours / BAKE 15–20 minutes

This is the French version of the focaccia — both names stem from the Latin *panis focacius*, which referred to bread baked in the hearth or fireplace. Fougasse is shallower and a little more crisp-crusted than a focaccia but has similar delicious qualities to its Italian counterpart and is equally suited to tearing and sharing. I like to serve it with a shallow dish of good extra virgin olive oil and balsamic vinegar (3 parts oil to 1 part vinegar) for dipping.

250g strong white bread flour, plus extra for dusting

5g salt

5g instant yeast

1 tbsp olive oil, plus extra to finish

190ml cool water

Fine semolina for dusting (optional)

Dried oregano to finish

1. Oil a 2–3 litre square plastic container.

2. Put the flour, salt and yeast into the bowl of a mixer fitted with a dough hook (don't put the salt directly on top of the yeast). Add the olive oil and three-quarters of the water. Begin mixing on a slow speed. As the dough starts to come together, add the remaining water slowly. Most flours should take the quantity of water stated, but you must add it slowly. Then mix for another 6–8 minutes on a medium speed. When ready, the dough should be very elastic and you should be able to stretch it away from the bowl.

3. Tip the dough into the prepared container. Cover and leave to rise until at least doubled in size — about 1 hour.

4. Line a baking tray with baking parchment or silicone paper.

5. After an hour the dough should be bouncy and shiny. Dust your work surface heavily with flour — add some semolina too, if you have some. Carefully tip out the dough onto the work surface; it will be very loose and flowing, but don't worry. Rather than knocking it back, handle it gently so you keep as much air in the dough as possible. Dust the top with flour and/or semolina.

6. Lift the dough onto the prepared baking tray and spread out with your fingers into a flat oval. Using a pizza cutter, make several 5cm long cuts in the dough, forming a leaf design, and then stretch the dough out to emphasise the holes.

7. Put the tray inside a clean plastic bag and leave to prove for 20 minutes. Meanwhile, heat your oven to 220°C.

8. Spray olive oil over the top of the loaf using a water spray bottle — or just trickle on the oil. Sprinkle oregano all over the surface. Bake for 15–20 minutes, or until the fougasse sounds hollow when tapped on the base. Cool on a wire rack and eat within a few hours of baking.

RYE BREAD

MAKES 1 loaf / PREP 8 hours / BAKE 30 minutes

Traditional in many Eastern European countries, this dark, pleasingly dense bread is full of earthy, nutty flavour. Serve it in thin slices with cheese or smoked fish. The black treacle is optional but it does add an extra layer of rich, sweet flavour.

500g rye flour, plus extra for dusting

10g salt

10g instant yeast

20ml black treacle (optional)

350ml cool water

Olive oil for kneading

1. Tip the flour into a large mixing bowl and add the salt to one side of the bowl and the yeast to the other. Add the treacle if using and three-quarters of the water, and turn the mixture round with your fingers. Continue to add the remaining water, a little at a time, until you've picked up all of the flour from the sides of the bowl. You may not need to add all the water, or you may need to add a little more – you want dough that is soft, but not soggy. Use the mixture to clean the inside of the bowl and keep going until the mixture forms a rough dough.

2. Coat the work surface with a little olive oil, then tip the dough onto it and begin to knead. Keep kneading for 5–10 minutes. Work through the initial wet stage until the dough starts to form a soft skin. You will find the dough feels different from a conventional wheat flour dough – less smooth and stretchy.

3. Put the dough into a lightly oiled large bowl. Cover with a tea towel and leave to rise until doubled in size – about 4 hours.

4. Tip the dough onto a lightly floured surface. Fold it repeatedly in on itself until the air is knocked out. Form the dough into a smooth, round cob by turning it on the surface and tucking the edges underneath until the top is smooth and tight (see pages 20–1). Generously dust the inside of a large, round proving basket (see page 30) with rye flour (or white flour). Put the dough into it, placing the smooth top side down.

5. Leave to prove for 2–3 hours; the dough will double in size eventually but will take considerably longer than wheat-flour breads. Meanwhile, heat your oven to 220°C and put a roasting tray in the bottom to heat up. Line a baking tray with parchment or silicone paper.

6. When your loaf is risen, invert it carefully onto the prepared tray. The basket should have left a pattern on the surface of the dough. Slash a deep crosshatch pattern on the top with a sharp knife. Pour hot water into the roasting tray to create steam and put the bread into the oven. Bake for 30 minutes. To test, tap the base of the loaf – it should sound hollow. Cool on a wire rack.

CHOLLA LOAF

MAKES 1 loaf / PREP 3 hours / BAKE 20–25 minutes

The recipe for this classic Jewish loaf was given to me by an old family friend, Sylvia Woolf. Despite the richness of the dough, the bread is very light, with a delicate sweetness from the sugar and milk. Traditionally served on the Sabbath, it is good at any time of the year for breakfast or tea, just sliced and buttered.

500g strong white
    bread flour, plus
    extra for dusting
10g salt
25g caster sugar
10g instant yeast
30g unsalted butter,
    softened
2 medium eggs, lightly
    beaten, plus an extra
    egg for glazing
50ml warm milk
180ml cool water

1. Tip the flour into a large mixing bowl and add the salt and sugar to one side of the bowl and the yeast to the other. Add the butter, the 2 beaten eggs and the milk, then half the water. Turn the mixture round with your fingers. Continue to add water, a little at a time, until you've picked up all the flour from the sides of the bowl. You may not need to add all the water, or you may need to add a little more — you want dough that is soft, but not soggy. Use the mixture to clean the inside of the bowl and keep going until the mixture forms a rough dough.

2. Lightly flour the work surface, then tip the dough onto it and begin to knead. Keep kneading for 5–10 minutes. Work through the initial wet stage until the dough starts to form a soft, smooth skin. Add a little flour if you need to, but don't overdo it.

3. When your dough feels smooth and silky, put it into a lightly oiled large bowl. Cover with a tea towel and leave to rise until at least doubled in size — at least 1 hour, but it's fine to leave it for 2 or even 3 hours.

4. Line a baking tray with baking parchment or silicone paper.

5. Tip the dough onto a lightly floured surface. Fold it inwards repeatedly until all the air is knocked out and the dough is smooth. Divide it into 3 equal pieces. Roll each piece out to a sausage, about 22cm long. Join the 3 pieces together at one end, ready to plait the strands. Start with the outer piece on the right and lift it over the middle piece, then lift the piece on the left over the middle, then the right over the middle and left over the middle. Repeat this sequence until you reach the end. Tuck the ends underneath to neaten. Lift the dough onto the prepared baking tray. Beat the remaining egg and brush over the top of the loaf.

6. Put the tray inside a clean plastic bag, making sure the bag doesn't touch the dough. Leave to prove for about 1 hour, or until the dough is at least doubled in size and springs back quickly if you prod it lightly with your finger. Meanwhile, heat your oven to 200°C.

7. Bake the loaf for 20–25 minutes or until it sounds hollow when tapped on the base. The loaf will colour quickly due to the sugar and egg, so keep an eye on it. Leave to cool on a wire rack.

CRUMPETS

MAKES about 20 / PREP 2½ hours / COOK 10 minutes per batch

Crumpets are cooked in a pan or on a griddle so this is not technically
baking, but given that the batter is leavened with yeast I've sneaked them in.
After all, I couldn't not give a recipe for crumpets — they are gorgeous!

450g plain flour
1 tsp caster sugar
14g instant yeast
350ml skimmed milk
350ml cold water
1 tsp salt
½ tsp bicarbonate
   of soda
A little sunflower oil
   for cooking

1. Sift the flour into a bowl and add the sugar and yeast. In a pan, heat the
   milk until just warm (about blood temperature, 37°C), then combine
   with the water. Beat the liquid into the flour to make a smooth batter.

2. Cover the bowl with cling film and leave the batter to stand at room
   temperature for 2 hours. It should more than double in size before
   dropping back down.

3. Beat the salt and bicarbonate of soda into the batter, then leave to rest
   for 10 minutes.

4. Heat a griddle or heavy frying pan over a low heat. Dab a little oil onto a
   piece of kitchen paper and rub over the inside of 4 metal crumpet rings,
   as well as the hot surface of the griddle or pan. Stand the rings on the
   griddle or in the pan.

5. Pour enough batter into each ring to half-fill it. Cook for 6–8 minutes
   or until the surface is set and filled with holes. Remove the rings and
   turn the crumpets over. Cook for a further 2–3 minutes — the first side
   should be well browned, the second only barely coloured. Repeat to
   cook the rest of the batter. Serve straight away or leave the crumpets to
   cool, then toast before eating.

FLAVO
BREA

HAVING COVERED BASIC BREADS, I want to show you how to introduce other ingredients into the dough, to change both the flavour and structure of the finished bread. I created some of these recipes while I was working in hotel kitchens, to complement their menus; others reflect time spent with my family. Several were inspired during my years in Cyprus, including the olive, onion and coriander loaf – bake it and your kitchen will be filled with the scents of that lovely country.

I hope you will want to try out your own ideas, using these recipes as templates. I have learnt over the years that if your basic dough is good, adding new flavours will almost always enhance it. It is, however, worth considering how ingredients can affect the dough. If, for example, you add olives to a base dough, they will release moisture as they are crushed by the kneading. To counter this, I add a little more flour to the dough. If you add acidic ingredients, such as onions, they can slow down the action of the yeast, so you'll need to allow extra time at the proving stage.

The more flavoured breads you bake, the more you will learn how to build and combine flavours.

TRUFFLE FICELLES

MAKES 6–8 / PREP 2 hours / BAKE 10–15 minutes

A ficelle is a kind of very thin baguette – *ficelle* means 'string' in French.
These crisp, open-textured little loaves are irresistible. Serve them with
pre-dinner drinks, soups and alongside almost any kind of salad.

**250g strong white
   bread flour, plus
   extra for dusting**

5g salt

5g instant yeast

200ml tepid water

1 tbsp olive oil

**Fine semolina for
   dusting (optional)**

To finish

**25ml truffle oil,
   mixed with 25ml
   olive oil**

Dried oregano

1. Oil a 2–3 litre square plastic container.

2. Put the flour into the bowl of a mixer fitted with a dough hook. Add
   the salt to one side of the bowl and the yeast to the other. Add three-
   quarters of the water and begin to mix on a slow speed. As the dough
   starts to come together, slowly add the remaining water. Then mix
   for a further 5–8 minutes on a medium speed. The dough should now
   be wet and stretch easily when pulled. Add the olive oil and mix for
   another 2 minutes.

3. Tip the dough into the oiled tub and leave until at least doubled in size
   – about 1 hour.

4. Line 2 baking trays with baking parchment or silicone paper.

5. Dust your work surface heavily with flour – add some semolina too,
   if you have some. Carefully tip the dough onto the surface – it will be
   very loose and flowing, but don't worry. Rather than knocking it back,
   handle it gently so keep as much air in the dough as possible. Coat
   the top of the dough with flour too, then pat it gently out to an even
   rectangle, 7–8cm deep. Starting at one long edge, cut the dough into
   6–8 strips. Stretch each piece out until about 25cm long.

6. Lay the dough strips on the prepared baking trays, spacing them apart,
   and make indentations along the length of each one with your fingers.
   Drizzle some of the truffle and olive oil mix along the top of each ficelle
   and sprinkle with a little oregano.

7. Put each tray inside a clean plastic bag and leave to prove for 30 minutes.
   Meanwhile, heat your oven to 230°C.

8. Bake the ficelles for 10–15 minutes. When they come out of the oven,
   sprinkle them with a little more of the oil mix. Leave to cool on a wire
   rack. Eat within 24 hours of baking.

PUMPKIN SEED STICKS WITH POPPY SEEDS

MAKES 10 / PREP 3 hours / BAKE 15–20 minutes

These crisp and crunchy breadsticks are great served as a pre-meal snack.
Alternatively, for a real treat, try dipping them into the melted interior
of an oven-baked whole small Brie or Camembert.

100g strong white bread flour, plus extra for dusting

200g strong wholemeal bread flour

200g malted bread flour

10g salt

10g instant yeast

30g unsalted butter, softened

340ml cool water

150g pumpkin seeds

50g poppy seeds

1. Put the flours into the bowl of a mixer fitted with a dough hook. Add the salt to one side of the bowl and the yeast to the other. Add the butter and three-quarters of the water and begin mixing on a slow speed. As the dough starts to come together, slowly add the remaining water. Mix for another 2 minutes on a slow speed, then 5 minutes on a medium speed. Add the pumpkin seeds and mix for a further 3 minutes.

2. Tip the dough into a lightly oiled large bowl, cover with a tea towel and leave until at least doubled in size — at least 1 hour.

3. Line 2 baking trays with baking parchment or silicone paper. Scatter the poppy seeds on a large board.

4. Tip the dough onto a lightly floured surface and fold it in on itself repeatedly until all the air is knocked out and the dough is smooth. Divide the dough into 10 pieces. Roll each piece out to a slim stick, about 30cm long. Brush with water and roll in the poppy seeds, then lay the dough sticks on the prepared baking trays, spacing them apart.

5. Put each tray inside a clean plastic bag and leave to prove for 1 hour, or until the dough is at least doubled in size and springs back quickly if you prod it lightly with your finger. Meanwhile, heat your oven to 220°C.

6. Bake the dough sticks for 15–20 minutes until golden brown and crisp. Leave to cool on a rack.

GREEN OLIVE STICKS

MAKES about 15 / PREP 2–3 hours / BAKE 10–15 minutes

These deeply savoury breadsticks are extraordinarily good. They are jam-packed with whole olives and very moreish indeed. You could use black rather than green olives if you like, for a different flavour. In order to hold all those olives, this dough is particularly wet, but do persevere with it — the results are more than worth it. Serve with pre-dinner drinks.

500g strong white bread flour, plus extra for dusting

10g salt

10g instant yeast

400ml tepid water

2 tbsp olive oil

500g good-quality pitted green olives, well drained

Fine semolina for dusting (optional)

1. Oil a 2–3 litre square plastic container.

2. Put the flour into the bowl of a mixer fitted with a dough hook. Add the salt to one side of the bowl and the yeast to the other. Add three-quarters of the water and begin mixing on a slow speed. As the dough starts to come together, slowly add the remaining water. Then mix for a further 5–8 minutes on a medium speed. The dough should now be wet and stretch easily when pulled. Add the olive oil and mix for a further 2 minutes. Add the olives and mix until well distributed.

3. Put the dough into the oiled tub and leave until at least tripled in size — at least 1 hour.

4. Line 3 or 4 baking trays with baking parchment or silicone paper.

5. Dust your work surface heavily with flour — add some semolina too, if you have some. Carefully tip the dough onto the surface. It will be very loose and flowing but don't worry. Rather than knocking it back, handle it gently so you keep as much air in the dough as possible. Dust the top of the dough with flour too, then stretch it out gently to a rough rectangle. Starting at one long edge, cut the dough into about 15 strips. Stretch each piece out until 20–25cm long. Put the strips onto the prepared baking trays, spacing them apart.

6. Put each tray inside a clean plastic bag and leave to prove for about 30 minutes. Meanwhile, heat your oven to 220°C.

7. Bake the dough sticks for 10–15 minutes. Cool on a wire rack.

MANEESH

MAKES 3 large or 10 small breads / PREP 2–3 hours / BAKE 15 minutes

I once baked these herby Middle Eastern breads for the great food writer, Claudia Roden. She liked them – praise indeed! They are particularly good served with dips of Greek or Lebanese origin, such as tzatziki, hummus and baba ganoush (aubergine dip), or any mezze-style food.

500g strong white bread flour, plus extra for dusting
10g salt
25g caster sugar
10g instant yeast
320ml tepid water
Olive oil for kneading and to finish

For the za'atar topping
6 tbsp sesame seeds
4 tbsp dried thyme
2 tbsp dried marjoram

1. Put the flour into a bowl and add the salt and sugar to one side of the bowl and the yeast to the other. Add three-quarters of the water and turn the mixture round with your fingers. Continue to add the remaining water, a little at a time, until you've picked up all the flour from the sides of the bowl. You may not need to add all the water, or you may need to add a little more – you want dough that is soft, but not soggy. Use the mixture to clean the inside of the bowl and keep going until the mixture forms a rough dough.

2. Coat your work surface with a little olive oil, then carefully tip the dough onto it and begin to knead. Keep kneading for 5–10 minutes. Work through the initial wet stage until the dough starts to form a soft, smooth skin.

3. When your dough feels smooth and silky, put it into a lightly oiled bowl. Cover with a tea towel and leave to rise until at least doubled in size – at least 1 hour, but it's fine to leave it for 2 or even 3 hours.

4. Line 3 or 4 baking trays with baking parchment or silicone paper.

5. Tip the dough onto a lightly oiled surface. Fold it in on itself repeatedly until all the air is knocked out and the dough is smooth. Either divide the dough into 3 equal pieces and roll each out to a large circle, about 30cm in diameter, or divide into 10 pieces and roll each piece between the palms of your hands until it is smooth and round, then flatten slightly. Place on the prepared baking trays.

6. Put each tray inside a clean plastic bag and leave to prove for about 20 minutes. Meanwhile, heat your oven to 230°C.

7. Brush the surface of the dough with a little olive oil. For the topping, mix the za'atar ingredients with enough olive oil to make a thick paste. Spread over the surface of the dough, then bake for 15 minutes. Cool on a wire rack.

STILTON AND GRAPE FLATBREADS

MAKES 12 / PREP 2 hours / COOK 5–6 minutes per flatbread

The layer of melted cheese in these delicious and unusual flatbreads gives them a rich, slightly flaky texture. I often serve them, still warm, with a selection of dips, such as tzatziki, guacamole and an aubergine dip.

500g strong white
    bread flour, plus
    extra for dusting
10g salt
10g instant yeast
30g unsalted butter,
    softened
310ml cool water
250g Stilton,
    crumbled
24 seedless green
    grapes, halved
Olive oil for cooking

1. Put the flour into a large bowl and add the salt to one side and the yeast to the other. Add the butter and three-quarters of the water and mix with your fingers to bring the ingredients together. Gradually add the remaining water, a little at a time, until you've picked up all the flour from the sides of the bowl. You may not need to add all the water, or you may need to add a little more – you want dough that is soft, but not soggy. Use the mixture to clean the inside of the bowl and keep going until the mixture forms a rough dough.

2. Tip the dough onto a lightly floured surface and begin to knead. Keep kneading for 5–10 minutes. Work through the initial wet stage until the dough starts to form a soft, smooth skin.

3. When your dough feels smooth and silky, put it into a lightly oiled bowl. Cover with a tea towel and leave to rise until at least doubled in size – at least 1 hour, but it's fine to leave it for 2 or even 3 hours.

4. Tip the dough onto a lightly floured surface. Fold it inwards repeatedly until all the air is knocked out and the dough is smooth. Divide the dough into 12 pieces and roll each piece into a ball.

5. Make an indentation in each ball and put about 20g of crumbled Stilton and 4 grape halves inside (1). Pinch the dough together over the filling to seal it in.

6. Press each filled dough ball gently with your hands (2) then roll it out with a rolling pin to a circle, about 18cm in diameter. The grapes will burst and leak a little juice as you do this but don't worry; use a little more flour to stop the dough sticking.

7. Heat a frying pan with a little olive oil over a medium-high heat. Fry each flatbread for 2–3 minutes on each side, until golden brown and puffy. Leave them to cool slightly on a wire rack, then serve.

FLATBREADS WITH EPOISSE AND BACON

MAKES 2 / PREP 1½ hours / COOK 30 minutes

I invented these luxurious flatbreads in the bakery one day when I had some leftover dough and plenty of rich, creamy Epoisse cheese to hand. They worked a treat! Serve them with something to balance their richness, such as a big green salad or a vegetable soup.

250g strong white
   bread flour, plus
   extra for dusting
5g instant yeast
5g salt
160ml cool water
Olive oil for kneading
   and cooking

For the topping
6 rashers of unsmoked
   back bacon, rind
   removed
150g Epoisse cheese

1. Put the flour into a mixing bowl. Add the yeast to one side of the bowl and the salt to the other. Add three-quarters of the water and mix with your fingers to bring the ingredients together. Gradually add the remaining water, a little at a time, until you've picked up all the flour from the sides of the bowl. You may not need to add all the water, or you may need to add a little more – you want dough that is soft, but not soggy. Use the mixture to clean the inside of the bowl and keep going until the mixture forms a rough dough.

2. Coat your work surface with a little olive oil, then carefully tip the dough onto it and begin to knead. Keep kneading for 5–10 minutes. Work through the initial wet stage until the dough starts to form a soft, smooth skin.

3. When your dough feels smooth and silky, put it into a lightly oiled bowl. Cover with a tea towel and leave to rise until at least doubled in size – at least 1 hour, but it's fine to leave it for 2 or even 3 hours.

4. Meanwhile, heat a dash of olive oil in a frying pan over a medium heat. Add the bacon and cook it gently on both sides (it will be cooked more later on). Remove the bacon with a slotted spoon and set aside, leaving the bacon fat in the frying pan.

5. Heat your oven to 200°C. Line a baking tray with baking parchment or silicone paper.

6. Tip the risen dough onto a lightly floured surface and fold it in on itself repeatedly until all the air is knocked out and the dough is smooth. Divide it into 2 pieces. Shape each piece into a ball, then use a rolling pin to roll it out to a circle, about 20cm in diameter.

7. Reheat the pan with the bacon fat over a medium-high heat. Add one of the flatbreads and cook for about 5 minutes each side. Repeat with the second flatbread, adding a dash more oil to the pan if necessary.

8. Put both flatbreads on the prepared baking tray. Top with the cheese, dividing it evenly between them, and lay 3 slices of bacon on each. Bake for 10 minutes until golden and the cheese is bubbling. Serve warm.

BREAKFAST ROLLS

MAKES 13–15 / PREP 2–3 hours / BAKE 15–20 minutes

These are breakfast rolls with a difference – the ingredients of a cooked breakfast are incorporated into the bread. You can vary the filling as you wish but this combination works very well. For a more virtuous breakfast bread, bake a muesli and banana sourdough (see page 155).

500g strong white bread flour, plus extra for dusting

10g salt

20g caster sugar

10g instant yeast

30g unsalted butter, softened

2 eggs, lightly beaten, plus an extra egg for glazing

250ml cool water

Olive oil for kneading and cooking

For the filling

10 rashers of unsmoked back bacon, rind removed

125ml tomato passata

100g button mushrooms, sliced

1. Tip the flour into a large mixing bowl and add the salt and sugar to one side of the bowl and the yeast to the other. Add the butter, beaten eggs and three-quarters of the water and turn the mixture round with your fingers. Continue to add the remaining water a little at a time, until you've picked up all the flour from the sides of the bowl. You may not need to add all the water, or you may need to add a little more – you want dough that is soft, but not soggy. Use the mixture to clean the inside of the bowl and keep going until the mixture forms a soft dough.

2. Coat the work surface with a little olive oil, then tip the dough onto it and begin to knead. Keep kneading for 5–10 minutes. Work through the initial wet stage until the dough starts to form a soft, smooth skin.

3. When your dough feels smooth and silky, put it into a lightly oiled bowl. Cover with a tea towel and leave to rise until at least doubled in size – at least 1 hour, but it's fine to leave it for 2 or even 3 hours.

4. Meanwhile, for the filling, heat a little olive oil in a frying pan over a medium heat. Add the bacon and cook gently on both sides until tender. Remove and set aside to cool.

5. Line 2 baking trays with baking parchment or silicone paper.

6. Tip the dough onto a lightly floured surface and, without knocking it back, roll it out to a rectangle about 35 x 30cm. With one long side towards you, spread a thin layer of passata over the dough and lay the bacon and mushrooms on top. Roll up the dough like a Swiss roll and press the join to seal. Cut into 13–15 pieces, each about 2.5cm long. Lay the rolls, flat side down, on the prepared baking trays, so they are close together.

7. Put each tray inside a clean plastic bag and leave to prove for 30 minutes. Meanwhile, heat your oven to 220°C.

8. Beat the remaining egg, brush over the dough and bake for 15–20 minutes until golden and cooked through. Eat warm.

GORGONZOLA, PEAR AND WALNUT BAKES

MAKES about 15 / PREP 3 hours / BAKE 15–20 minutes

These fabulous rolls, combining 'the big three flavourings' – nuts, cheese and fruit – are perfect for a party snack or lunch, and excellent with soups. You can substitute apple for the pear if you wish.

500g strong white
   bread flour, plus
   extra for dusting
10g salt
10g instant yeast
20g unsalted butter,
   softened
300ml cool water
230g Gorgonzola
   cheese
100g walnut halves
2 large pears, peeled,
   cored and thickly
   sliced

1. Tip the flour into a large mixing bowl and add the salt to one side of the bowl and the yeast to the other. Add the butter and three-quarters of the water and turn the mixture round with your fingers. Continue to add the remaining water, a little at a time, until you've picked up all of the flour from the sides of the bowl. You may not need to add all of the water, or you may need to add a little more – you want dough that is soft, but not soggy. Use the mixture to clean the inside of the bowl and keep going until the mixture forms a rough dough.

2. Tip the dough onto a lightly floured surface and begin to knead. Keep kneading for 5–10 minutes. Work through the initial wet stage until the dough starts to form a soft, smooth skin.

3. When your dough feels smooth and silky, put it into a lightly oiled bowl. Cover with a tea towel and leave to rise until at least doubled in size – at least 1 hour, but it's fine to leave it for 2 or even 3 hours.

4. Line 2 baking trays with baking parchment or silicone paper.

5. Tip the dough onto a lightly floured surface. Without knocking the dough back first, use a rolling pin to roll it out into a rectangle, about 2.5cm thick. Turn the dough 90° if necessary, so you have a long edge facing you. Tack this closest edge to the work surface with your fingers.

6. Crumble or spread the cheese all over the top of the dough, then smash up your walnuts and sprinkle them over the cheese. Roll up the dough towards you to form a long sausage. Now lift the tacked bit into the sausage and roll the lot on the table to make sure the dough sticks together. You should now have a sausage filled with walnuts and cheese. Cut the sausage into 3cm pieces and lay them, flat side down, on the prepared baking trays, spacing them apart.

7. Put each tray inside a clean plastic bag and leave to prove for 30 minutes, or until the dough is doubled in size and springs back quickly if you prod it lightly with your finger. Meanwhile, heat your oven to 220°C.

8. When the little rolls have risen, press a piece of pear into each – if you think you can fit two pieces in each, go for it. Sprinkle with flour and bake for 15–20 minutes until golden and cooked through. Enjoy warm.

GARLIC BREAD

MAKES 2 loaves / PREP 3 hours / BAKE 25 minutes

Enticingly aromatic from the whole roasted garlic cloves baked within the
dough, this is real garlic bread. It's a great accompaniment to soups and
antipasti, as well as grilled or barbecued meats and vegetables.

500g strong white
   bread flour, plus
   extra for dusting
10g salt, plus a little
   extra for the garlic
10g instant yeast
30g unsalted butter,
   softened
320ml cool water

For the roasted garlic
3 garlic bulbs,
   broken into cloves
1 tbsp olive oil
1 tsp caster sugar

To finish
Olive oil for
   sprinkling
Dried oregano

1. Tip the flour into a large mixing bowl and add the salt to one side of
the bowl and the yeast to the other. Add the butter and three-quarters
of the water and turn the mixture round with your fingers. Continue
to add water, a little at a time, until you've picked up all the flour from
the sides of the bowl. You may not need to add all the water, or you may
need to add a little more — you want dough that is soft, but not soggy.
Use the mixture to clean the inside of the bowl and keep going until the
mixture forms a rough dough.

2. Tip the dough onto a lightly floured work surface and begin to knead.
Keep kneading for 5–10 minutes. Work through the initial wet stage
until the dough starts to form a soft, smooth skin.

3. When your dough feels smooth and silky, put it into a lightly oiled bowl.
Cover with a tea towel and leave to rise until at least doubled in size —
at least 1 hour, but it's fine to leave it for 2 or even 3 hours.

4. Meanwhile, for the roasted garlic, heat your oven to 200°C. Peel the
garlic cloves, put them in a roasting dish and sprinkle with a little salt,
the olive oil and sugar. Roast for 20 minutes until golden brown and
soft to the touch — this releases the flavour of the garlic. Leave to cool.

5. Line 2 baking trays with baking parchment or silicone paper.

6. Add the whole roasted garlic cloves to the risen dough and knead in
well. Tip the dough onto a lightly floured surface. Divide the dough
into 2 pieces and stretch each piece out to an oblong, about 22cm long.
Place each loaf on a baking tray.

7. Put each tray inside a clean plastic bag and leave to prove for 1 hour, or
until the dough is at least doubled in size and springs back quickly if you
prod it lightly with your finger. Meanwhile, heat your oven to 220°C.

8. Once risen, sprinkle the loaves with olive oil and then oregano. Bake for
25 minutes or until they sound hollow when tapped on the base. Cool
on a wire rack.

CORIANDER, OLIVE AND ONION BREAD

MAKES 1 loaf / PREP 3–4 hours / BAKE 30 minutes

This hearty, crusty loaf is one of my personal favourites, as it was inspired by my time working in Cyprus. You will come across a version of it in villages all over the island. It is lovely with a cucumber or aubergine dip and olives, but my favourite way to eat it is to smear a slice with a ripe avocado and top it with slices of fresh, flavourful tomato and a squeeze of lemon juice.

500g strong white bread flour, plus extra for dusting

10g salt

10g instant yeast

40ml olive oil, plus extra for kneading

300ml cool water

A handful of chopped coriander

1 onion, peeled and finely chopped

200g good-quality, pitted black olives, roughly chopped

For the seed mix

80g sesame seeds

10g black cumin seeds

10g nigella (kalonji) seeds

1. Tip the flour into a large mixing bowl and add the salt to one side of the bowl and the yeast to the other. Add the olive oil and three-quarters of the water and turn the mixture round with your fingers. Continue to add the remaining water, a little at a time, until you've picked up all the flour from the sides of the bowl. You may not need to add all the water, or you may need to add a little more — you want dough that is soft, but not soggy. Use the mixture to clean the inside of the bowl and keep going until the mixture forms a rough dough.

2. Coat your work surface with a little olive oil, then tip the dough onto it and begin to knead. Keep kneading for 5–10 minutes. Work through the initial wet stage until the dough starts to form a soft, smooth skin.

3. When your dough feels smooth and silky, put it into a lightly oiled bowl. Cover with a tea towel and leave to rise until at least doubled in size — at least 1 hour, but it's fine to leave it for 2 or even 3 hours.

4. Tip the dough onto a lightly floured surface. Add the coriander, onion and olives and knead them in until evenly distributed throughout the dough. There is a lot to be incorporated but keep going — it will get easier as you knead. The aroma will be fantastic at this point.

5. Put the dough back into a bowl, cover and leave to rise again for another 30 minutes.

6. Line a baking tray with baking parchment or silicone paper.

7. Tip the dough onto a floured surface and flatten it with your hands into a rough rectangle, then roll it up into a sausage. Combine the sesame, cumin and nigella seeds. Brush the dough with a little warm water, then sprinkle all over with the seed mix. Put the dough onto the baking tray and snip into the top deeply with scissors.

8. Put the tray inside a clean plastic bag and leave to prove for 1 hour, or until the dough is at least doubled in size and springs back quickly if you prod it lightly with your finger. Meanwhile, heat your oven to 220°C.

9. Bake the loaf for 30 minutes or until it sounds hollow when tapped on the base. Cool on a wire rack.

SEEDED BREAD

MAKES 1 loaf / PREP 3–4 hours / BAKE 30 minutes

This recipe is dedicated to my mother-in-law, Gloria, as it is a firm favourite of hers. A perfect everyday bread packed with nutrients and flavour, it's also exceptionally good toasted and served with cheese.

300g strong wholemeal bread flour

100g rye flour

100g strong white bread flour, plus extra for dusting

10g salt

10g instant yeast

2 tbsp black treacle

340ml cool water

For the seed mix

80g sunflower seeds

80g pumpkin seed

20g poppy seeds

40g sesame seeds

60g linseed

40g millet seed

To finish

40g sesame seeds

1. Put the flours into the bowl of a mixer fitted with a dough hook. Add the salt to one side of the bowl and the yeast to the other. Add the treacle and three-quarters of the water, and begin mixing on a slow speed. As the dough starts to come together, slowly add the remaining water. Then mix for a further 7 minutes on medium speed. For the seed mix, combine the seeds and add them to the dough. Mix for 2 minutes on a slow speed (you might need to work the last of the seeds in by hand). Take out the dough hook.

2. Cover the bowl and leave the dough to rise until at least doubled in size – this should take around 2 hours, but it's fine to leave it for 3 hours.

3. Line a baking tray with baking parchment or silicone paper.

4. Tip the dough onto a lightly floured surface and fold it in on itself repeatedly until all the air is knocked out and the dough is smooth. Shape the dough into an oval (see page 23), brush with a little warm water, then sprinkle with the sesame seeds. Transfer to your baking tray and slash down the length of the stick with a sharp knife.

5. Put the tray inside a clean plastic bag and leave to prove for 1 hour, or until the dough is at least doubled in size and springs back quickly if you prod it lightly with your finger. Meanwhile, heat your oven to 230°C.

6. Once the dough is risen, bake for 30 minutes or until the loaf sounds hollow when tapped on the base. Leave to cool on a wire rack.

CHERRY TOMATO AND MOZZARELLA BREADS

MAKES 4 / PREP 2 hours / BAKE 15–20 minutes

These luscious breads are delicious eaten still warm. However, if you can't serve them straight after baking, they can be reheated in your oven at 220°C for 5 minutes. Drizzle the loaves with a little olive oil as you take them out of the oven.

500g strong white bread flour, plus extra for dusting

10g salt

10g instant yeast

400ml tepid water

2 tbsp olive oil, plus extra for sprinkling

Fine semolina for dusting (optional)

20 cherry tomatoes, halved

2 balls of buffalo mozzarella, about 125g each

Dried oregano for sprinkling

1. Oil a 2–3 litre square plastic container.

2. Put the flour into the bowl of a mixer fitted with a dough hook. Add the salt to one side of the bowl and the yeast to the other. Add three-quarters of the water and begin mixing on a slow speed. As the dough begins to come together, slowly add the remaining water. Mix for a further 5–8 minutes on a medium speed. The dough should now be wet and stretch easily when pulled. Add the olive oil and mix for another 2 minutes.

3. Put the dough into the oiled tub, cover and leave until at least doubled in size – about 1 hour.

4. Line 2 baking trays with baking parchment or silicone paper.

5. Dust your work surface heavily with flour – add some semolina too, if you have some. Tip the dough out carefully onto the surface. Rather than knocking it back, handle it gently so you keep as much air in the dough as possible. Coat the top with flour too. Cut the dough in half lengthways, then cut each half across in two to give 4 pieces of dough.

6. Stretch each piece of dough a little and lay two breads on each prepared tray, spacing them apart. Push 10 tomato halves into the surface of each bread. Tear the mozzarella into little pieces and push them in between the tomatoes. Sprinkle each bread with olive oil, then oregano. Leave to rest for 15 minutes. Meanwhile, heat your oven to 210°C.

7. Bake the breads for 15–20 minutes. Serve while still warm.

BACON AND CHEDDAR LOAVES

MAKES 4 / PREP 3 hours / BAKE 20 minutes

These are an absolute winner with kids. My boy Joshua, given the chance,
would eat them for breakfast, lunch and dinner.

400g strong white
 bread flour, plus
 extra for dusting

100g strong wholemeal
 bread flour

10g salt

10g instant yeast

30g unsalted butter,
 softened

330ml cool water

For the filling

Olive oil for cooking
 and to finish

8 rashers of smoked
 back bacon, rind
 removed

150g Cheddar, grated

1. Tip the flours into a large mixing bowl and add the salt to one side of the bowl and the yeast to the other. Add the butter and three-quarters of the water and turn the mixture round with your fingers. Continue to add the remaining water, a little at a time, until you've picked up all the flour from the sides of the bowl. You may not need to add all the water, or you may need to add a little more – you want dough that is soft, but not soggy. Use the mixture to clean the inside of the bowl and keep going until the mixture forms a rough dough.

2. Tip the dough onto a lightly floured surface and begin to knead. Keep kneading for 5–10 minutes. Work through the initial wet stage until the dough starts to form a soft, smooth skin.

3. When your dough feels smooth and silky, put it into a lightly oiled bowl. Cover with a tea towel and leave to rise until at least doubled in size – at least 1 hour, but it's fine to leave it for 2 or even 3 hours.

4. Meanwhile, for the filling, heat a little olive oil in a frying pan over a medium heat. Add the bacon and cook gently on both sides until tender. Remove and set aside to cool, then chop.

5. Line 2 baking trays with baking parchment or silicone paper.

6. Once the dough is risen, add the bacon and cheese to it and knead in until well distributed. Tip the dough onto a lightly floured surface and knead briefly, pushing any pieces of bacon or cheese that bounce out back in.

7. Divide the dough into 4 pieces and shape into ovals, about 2.5cm thick (see page 23), tapering the ends of the loaves into points. Place 2 dough ovals on each tray, spacing them apart. Dust the loaves with flour and deeply slash the tops lengthways.

8. Put each tray inside a clean plastic bag and leave to prove for 1 hour, or until the dough is at least doubled in size and springs back quickly if you prod it lightly with your finger. Meanwhile, heat your oven to 220°C.

9. Sprinkle the loaves with a little olive oil and bake for 20 minutes until golden brown. Eat warm.

CHEDDAR AND APPLE BREAD

MAKES I loaf / PREP 3 hours / BAKE 30 minutes

Cheese and apple make a great combination alongside good bread, but
they are just as good if you put them into the loaf itself. Serve it warm with
a steaming bowl of soup on a cold day.

500g strong white
    bread flour, plus
    extra for dusting
10g salt
10g instant yeast
300ml cool water
Olive oil for kneading
150g Cheddar, grated
2 dessert apples,
    peeled, cored
    and sliced

1. Tip the flour into a large mixing bowl and add the salt to one side
   of the bowl and the yeast to the other. Add three-quarters of the water
   and turn the mixture round with your fingers. Continue to add the
   remaining water, a little at a time, until you've picked up all the flour
   from the sides of the bowl. You may not need to add all the water, or
   you may need to add a little more — you want dough that is soft, but not
   soggy. Use the mixture to clean the inside of the bowl and keep going
   until the mixture forms a rough dough.

2. Coat the work surface with a little olive oil, then tip the dough onto it
   and begin to knead. Keep kneading for 5–10 minutes. Work through
   the initial wet stage until the dough starts to form a soft, smooth skin.

3. When your dough feels smooth and silky, put it into a lightly oiled large
   bowl. Cover with a tea towel and leave to rise until at least doubled in
   size — at least 1 hour, but it's fine to leave it for 2 or even 3 hours.

4. Line a baking tray with baking parchment or silicone paper.

5. When the dough is ready, tip it onto a lightly floured surface and gently
   squash it down into a rectangle, 2–3cm deep and twice as long as it is
   wide. Cover half the dough with the grated cheese and apple, leaving
   a clear margin around the edge, then fold the rest of the dough over to
   make a square parcel. Seal the edges. Put the dough onto the prepared
   baking tray.

6. Put the tray inside a clean plastic bag and leave to prove for 1 hour, or
   until the dough is at least doubled in size and springs back quickly if you
   prod it lightly with your finger. Meanwhile, heat your oven to 220°C.

7. Dust the loaf with flour and make deep imprints with your fingertips all
   over the dough, going right down to the tray. Bake for 30 minutes until
   golden brown. Cool on a wire rack. Serve warm or cold, sliced or torn.

STILTON AND PECAN TWIST

MAKES 1 loaf / PREP 3 hours / BAKE 30 minutes

I always find Stilton works brilliantly in breads — its strong flavour carries well, while its slight bitterness is offset by the soft, wheaty taste of the crumb. This handsome twist is great with cold meats and salads.

500g strong white bread flour, plus extra for dusting

10g salt

10g instant yeast

30g unsalted butter, softened

320ml cool water

Olive oil for kneading

200g Stilton, crumbled

150g pecan nuts

1. Tip the flour into a large mixing bowl and add the salt to one side of the bowl and the yeast to the other. Add the butter and three-quarters of the water and turn the mixture round with your fingers. Continue to add the remaining water, a little at a time, until you've picked up all the flour from the sides of the bowl. You may not need to add all the water, or you may need to add a little more — you want dough that is soft, but not soggy. Use the mixture to clean the inside of the bowl and keep going until the mixture forms a rough dough.

2. Coat the work surface with a little olive oil, then tip the dough onto it and begin to knead. Keep kneading for 5–10 minutes. Work through the initial wet stage until the dough starts to form a soft, smooth skin.

3. When your dough feels smooth and silky, put it into a lightly oiled bowl. Cover with a tea towel and leave to rise until at least doubled in size — at least 1 hour, but it's fine to leave it for 2 or even 3 hours.

4. Line a baking tray with baking parchment or silicone paper.

5. Add the Stilton and whole pecans to the dough and work them well in. Tip the dough out onto a lightly floured surface and divide it in two. Roll each piece into a sausage, about 30cm long. Now twist the two together — I do this by holding them together at one end and spinning them. Put the dough onto the prepared baking tray.

6. Put the tray inside a clean plastic bag and leave to prove for 1 hour, or until the dough is at least doubled in size and springs back quickly if you prod it lightly with your finger. Meanwhile, heat your oven to 220°C.

7. Dust the twist with flour and bake for 30 minutes. When ready, it will sound hollow when tapped on the base. Cool on a wire rack.

CRANBERRY AND STILTON BREAD

MAKES 1 loaf / PREP 3 hours / BAKE 30 minutes

If you want a change from cheese and biscuits at Christmas, give this
flavoursome bread a try. To be honest, though, it tastes great at any time
of year, and always goes well with a cheese board.

**500g strong white
bread flour, plus
extra for dusting**

10g salt

10g instant yeast

**30g unsalted butter,
softened**

320ml cool water

**100g dried
cranberries**

**150g Stilton,
crumbled**

1. Tip the flour into a large mixing bowl and add the salt to one side of
   the bowl and the yeast to the other. Add the butter and three-quarters
   of the water and turn the mixture round with your fingers. Continue to
   add the remaining water, a little at a time, until you've picked up all the
   flour from the sides of the bowl. You may not need to add all the water,
   or you may need to add a little more – you want dough that is soft, but
   not soggy. Use the mixture to clean the inside of the bowl and keep
   going until the mixture forms a rough dough.

2. Tip the dough out onto a lightly floured surface and begin to knead.
   Keep kneading for 5–10 minutes. Work through the initial wet stage
   until the dough starts to form a soft, smooth skin.

3. When your dough feels smooth and silky, put it into a lightly oiled bowl.
   Cover with a tea towel and leave to rise until at least doubled in size –
   at least 1 hour, but it's fine to leave it for 2 or even 3 hours.

4. Line a baking tray with baking parchment or silicone paper.

5. Tip your dough out onto a lightly floured surface. Without knocking it
   back, flatten it out with your hands, then roll out using a rolling pin
   into a rectangle, about 35 x 25cm. Turn the dough 90° if necessary, so
   you have a long edge facing you. Sprinkle the cranberries and Stilton on
   top as evenly as you can. Roll the dough up from the closest edge into a
   sausage. Press along the seam to seal it. Coil the sausage into a spiral and
   put it on the prepared baking tray.

6. Put the tray inside a clean plastic bag and leave to prove for 1 hour, or
   until the dough is at least doubled in size and springs back quickly if you
   prod it lightly with your finger. Meanwhile, heat your oven to 220°C
   and put a roasting tray in the bottom to heat up.

7. When the dough is risen and feels light to the touch, fill the roasting
   tray with hot water and put the bread in the middle of the oven. Bake
   for 30 minutes or until the loaf sounds hollow when tapped on the base.
   Cool on a wire rack.

PECAN LOAF

MAKES 1 loaf / PREP 3 hours / BAKE 35 minutes

I designed this loaf with your cheeseboard in mind. The stronger the cheese you serve with this dark, nutty bread, the better. Toasted and served with a mature Cheddar, it is fantastic. The quantity of pecans seems a lot when you are adding them – but don't worry, they spread themselves nicely through the rising dough. In fact, if you really like pecans, you could add even more – the dough can take it.

100g rye flour

300g strong wholemeal bread flour

100g strong white bread flour, plus extra for dusting

10g salt

10g instant yeast

30g unsalted butter, softened

2 tbsp black treacle

350ml water

240g pecan nuts

1. Put the flours into the bowl of a mixer fitted with a dough hook. Add the salt to one side of the bowl and the yeast to the other. Add the butter, treacle and three-quarters of the water and begin mixing on a slow speed. As the dough starts to come together, slowly add the remaining water. Mix slowly for 4 minutes, then on a medium speed for another 5 minutes. Add the pecans and mix on a slow speed for 1 minute to blend in the nuts and smash them up a little. Remove the dough hook.

2. Cover the bowl and leave until the dough is at least doubled in size – at least 1 hour, but it's fine to leave it for 2 or even 3 hours.

3. Line a baking tray with baking parchment or silicone paper.

4. Tip the dough onto a lightly floured surface and fold it in on itself repeatedly until all the air is knocked out. Flatten out into a rectangle. Roll it up into a sausage, then flatten out the dough again and roll it up a bit tighter this time. The dough should be about 30cm long. Tuck the edges underneath and neaten by rolling the edges to taper them slightly. Put the dough onto the prepared baking tray, with the join underneath.

5. Put the tray inside a clean plastic bag and leave to prove for 1 hour, or until the dough is at least doubled in size and springs back quickly if you prod it lightly with your finger. Meanwhile, heat your oven to 210°C.

6. Rub flour lightly all over the loaf, then make deep cuts on the diagonal along the loaf, first in one direction then the other, to make a criss-cross pattern. Bake for 35 minutes. The finished loaf will be quite dark because of the treacle. It will sound hollow when tapped on the base when it is ready. Cool on a wire rack.

FRUIT LOAF

MAKES 2 loaves / PREP 3 hours / BAKE 20 minutes

Packed with fruit and spiked with cinnamon and lemon zest, this delicious
sweet loaf is fantastic sliced and spread with butter. It is a fairly rich, sticky
dough so I recommend using an electric mixer.

500g strong white
flour, plus extra
for dusting

10g salt

10g instant yeast

40g unsalted butter,
softened

50g caster sugar

3 medium eggs,
lightly beaten

160ml warm full-fat
milk

160ml cool water

100g sultanas

80g raisins

60g ready-to-eat dried
apricots, chopped

60g chopped mixed
peel

½ tsp ground
cinnamon

For the icing

100g icing sugar,
sifted

Finely grated zest of
1 lemon

2–3 tsp water

1. Put the flour into the bowl of a mixer fitted with a dough hook. Add the salt to one side of the bowl and the yeast to the other. Add the butter, sugar, eggs, milk and half the water and begin mixing on a slow speed. As the dough starts to come together, slowly add the remaining water. Carry on mixing on a medium speed for 5 minutes. The dough should be elastic and soft to touch. If it still looks unmixed or breaks easily when you tug it, mix it for a further 2 minutes. Add all the dried fruits, mixed peel and cinnamon and mix again for 2 minutes.

2. Cover the bowl and leave the dough to rise until at least doubled in size — at least 1 hour, but it's fine to leave it for 2 or even 3 hours.

3. Line 2 baking trays with baking parchment or silicone paper.

4. Tip the dough onto a lightly floured surface. Fold it inwards repeatedly until all the air is knocked out and the dough is smooth, then divide into 2 pieces. Shape each piece into a ball and put each ball onto a prepared baking tray.

5. Put each tray inside a clean plastic bag and leave to prove for 1 hour, or until the dough is at least doubled in size and springs back quickly if you prod it lightly with your finger. Meanwhile, heat your oven to 210°C.

6. When the dough is ready, bake for 20 minutes or until the loaves sound hollow when tapped on the base. Transfer to a wire rack.

7. For the icing, put the icing sugar and lemon zest in a small bowl and slowly whisk in the water, a few drops at a time, until the mixture is the consistency of a batter. Brush this mixture over the top of each warm loaf and leave to cool.

APRICOT, DATE AND SULTANA LOAF

MAKES I loaf / PREP 4 hours / BAKE 35 minutes

This loaf is brimming with flavour from the rye flour, while the dates add a chewy, sweet and earthy element to the mix. It's an excellent bread for the cheeseboard and equally good toasted for breakfast.

300g strong white bread flour, plus extra for dusting

100g rye flour

100g strong wholemeal bread flour

10g salt

10g instant yeast

30g unsalted butter, softened

20ml black treacle

320ml cool water

Vegetable oil for kneading

100g sultanas

80g dates, chopped

100g ready-to-eat dried apricots, chopped

1. Tip the flours into a large mixing bowl and add the salt to one side of the bowl and the yeast to the other. Add the butter, treacle and three-quarters of the water and turn the mixture round with your fingers. Continue to add the water, a little at a time, until you've picked up all the flour from the sides of the bowl. You may not need to add all the water, or you may need to add a little more – you want dough that is soft, but not soggy. Use the mixture to clean the inside of the bowl and keep going until the mixture forms a rough dough.

2. Coat the work surface with a little vegetable oil, then tip the dough onto it and begin to knead. Keep kneading for 5–10 minutes. Work through the initial wet stage until the dough starts to form a soft, smooth skin.

3. When your dough feels smooth and silky, put it into a lightly oiled large bowl. Cover with a tea towel and leave to rise until at least doubled in size – at least 1 hour, but it's fine to leave it for 2 or even 3 hours.

4. Tip the dough onto a lightly floured surface. Add the sultanas, dates and apricots and knead them in. Put the dough back in the bowl, cover and leave to rise for a further hour.

5. Line a baking tray with baking parchment or silicone paper.

6. Tip the risen dough onto a lightly floured surface. Fold it inwards repeatedly until all the air is knocked out and the dough is smooth. Now shape the dough into an oval (see page 23) and place on the prepared baking tray.

7. Put the tray inside a clean plastic bag and leave to prove for 1 hour, or until the dough is at least doubled in size and springs back quickly if you prod it lightly with your finger. Meanwhile, heat your oven to 210°C.

8. Gently rub flour all over the dough and cut a deep slash along the length of the loaf. Bake for 35 minutes, or until the bread sounds hollow when tapped on the base. Cool on a wire rack.

TEACAKES

MAKES 8 / PREP 3 hours / BAKE 15 minutes

These large, soft, sweet and fruity teacakes are quite different from their shop-bought counterparts, which can have a dry, cotton-woolly texture and disappointing flavour. They are very good when they've just come out of the oven, but even better the next day — split, toasted and slathered in butter.

500g strong white bread flour, plus extra for dusting

10g salt

60g caster sugar

1 tsp ground cinnamon

10g instant yeast

50g unsalted butter, softened

300ml cool water

Vegetable oil for kneading

100g sultanas

100g chopped mixed peel

1 egg, beaten, to glaze

1. Tip the flour into a large mixing bowl and add the salt, sugar and cinnamon to one side of the bowl and the yeast to the other. Add the butter and three-quarters of the water, and turn the mixture round with your fingers. Continue to add the water, a little at a time, until you've picked up all the flour from the sides of the bowl. You may not need to add all the water, or you may need to add a little more — you want dough that is soft, but not soggy. Use the mixture to clean the inside of the bowl and keep going until the mixture forms a rough dough.

2. Coat the work surface with a little vegetable oil, then tip the dough onto it and begin to knead. Keep kneading for 5–10 minutes. Work through the initial wet stage until the dough starts to form a soft, smooth skin.

3. When your dough feels smooth and silky, put it into a large, lightly oiled bowl. Cover with a tea towel and leave to rise until at least doubled in size — at least 1 hour, but it's fine to leave it for 2 or even 3 hours.

4. Line 2 baking trays with baking parchment or silicone paper.

5. Tip the sultanas and mixed peel on top of the risen dough in the bowl and start working them into it. After a minute or two, tip the dough out onto a lightly floured surface and knead until the fruit is thoroughly mixed in.

6. Divide the dough into 8 pieces. Shape each into a ball, then use a rolling pin to flatten each one out to a round bun, about 1cm thick. Brush the teacakes with the beaten egg. Transfer to the prepared baking trays, spacing them apart.

7. Put each tray inside a clean plastic bag and leave to rise for about an hour until the teacakes are at least doubled in size. Meanwhile, heat your oven to 200°C.

8. Bake the teacakes for 10–15 minutes until risen and golden. Cool on a wire rack.

HOT CROSS BUNS

MAKES 12 / PREP 4 hours / BAKE 20 minutes

Packed with flavour, these are real hot cross buns. I started making them
with my dad, also a baker, when I was just nine years old. The addition
of apples to the dough enhances the taste and lends a lovely, moist texture.

**500g strong white
  bread flour, plus
  extra for dusting**

10g salt

75g caster sugar

10g instant yeast

**40g unsalted butter,
  softened**

2 medium eggs, beaten

**120ml warm full-fat
  milk**

120ml cool water

150g sultanas

**80g chopped mixed
  peel**

**Finely grated zest of
  2 oranges**

**1 dessert apple, cored
  and diced**

**2 tsp ground
  cinnamon**

For the crosses
75g plain flour
75ml water

For the glaze
75g apricot jam

1. Put the flour into a large mixing bowl. Add the salt and sugar to one
   side of the bowl and the yeast to the other. Add the butter, eggs, milk
   and half the water and turn the mixture round with your fingers.
   Continue to add the water, a little at a time, until you've picked up all
   the flour from the sides of the bowl. You may not need to add all the
   water, or you may need to add a little more – you want dough that is
   soft, but not soggy. Use the mixture to clean the inside of the bowl and
   keep going until the mixture forms a rough dough.

2. Tip the dough onto a lightly floured surface and begin to knead. Keep
   kneading for 5–10 minutes. Work through the initial wet stage until the
   dough starts to form a soft, smooth skin.

3. When your dough feels smooth and silky, put it into a lightly oiled large
   bowl. Cover with a tea towel and leave to rise until at least doubled in
   size – at least 1 hour, but it's fine to leave it for 2 or even 3 hours.

4. Tip the dough onto a lightly floured surface and scatter the sultanas,
   mixed peel, orange zest, apple and cinnamon on top. Knead in until
   evenly incorporated (1). Cover and leave to rise for a further hour.

5. Fold the dough inwards repeatedly until all the air is knocked out. Divide into 12 pieces ② and roll into balls. Place, fairly close together, on 1 or 2 baking trays lined with baking parchment or silicone paper.

6. Put each tray inside a clean plastic bag and leave to rest for 1 hour, or until the dough is at least doubled in size and springs back quickly if you prod it lightly with your finger. Meanwhile, heat your oven to 220°C.

7. For the crosses, mix the flour and water to a paste. Using a piping bag fitted with a fine nozzle, pipe crosses on the buns. Bake for 20 minutes, or until golden brown. Warm the apricot jam with a splash of water, sieve and brush over the tops of the warm buns to glaze. Cool on a wire rack.

1

2

3

APRICOT COURONNE

MAKES 1 loaf / PREP 3 hours / BAKE 25 minutes

A couronne, or 'crown', is a traditional French Christmas loaf. I've been making these rich sweet breads — stuffed with marzipan, fruit and nuts — for years. Believe me, they are well worth a try. They make a wonderful centrepiece to a Christmas feast, or a spectacular gift.

250g strong white
bread flour, plus
extra for dusting
5g salt
8g instant yeast
50g unsalted butter,
softened, plus extra
for greasing
135ml warm full-fat
milk
1 medium egg, lightly
beaten

For the filling
120g ready-to-eat
dried apricots,
chopped
150ml orange juice
(freshly squeezed
or from a carton)
90g unsalted butter,
softened
70g light muscovado
sugar
35g plain flour
60g raisins
65g chopped walnuts
Finely grated zest of
1 orange
200g marzipan
(see page 252), or
use ready-made

To finish
50g apricot jam
100g icing sugar
50g flaked almonds

1. The night before, for the filling, put the apricots into a bowl, pour on the orange juice and set aside to macerate.

2. The next day, tip the flour into a large mixing bowl and add the salt to one side of the bowl and the yeast to the other. Add the butter, milk and egg and turn the mixture round with your fingers. Continue to mix until you've picked up all the flour from the sides of the bowl. Use the mixture to clean the inside of the bowl and keep going until you have a soft dough.

3. Tip the dough onto a lightly floured surface and begin to knead. Keep kneading for about 6 minutes. Work through the initial wet stage until the dough starts to form a soft, smooth skin.

4. When your dough feels smooth and silky, put it into a lightly oiled bowl. Cover with a tea towel and leave to rise until at least doubled in size — at least 1 hour, but it's fine to leave it for 2 or even 3 hours.

5. While the dough is rising, make the filling. Drain the apricots. Cream the butter and muscovado sugar together in a bowl until light and fluffy. Mix in the drained apricots, flour, raisins, walnuts and orange zest.

6. Line a baking tray with baking parchment or silicone paper.

7. Turn the risen dough onto a lightly floured surface. Without knocking it back, roll out the dough into a rectangle, about 33 x 25cm. Turn the dough 90° if necessary, so you have a long edge facing you. Spread the apricot mixture evenly over the dough. On a floured surface, roll out the marzipan thinly and lay it over the apricot mixture. Roll up the dough tightly like a Swiss roll ①. Roll it slightly to seal, then cut it almost in half lengthways, leaving it just joined at one end — like a pair of legs ②. Twist the 2 dough lengths together ③, then join the ends to form a circular 'crown'. Transfer to the baking tray.

8. Put the tray inside a clean plastic bag and leave to prove for 1 hour, or until the dough is at least doubled in size and springs back quickly if you prod it lightly with your finger. Meanwhile, heat your oven to 200°C.

9. Bake the couronne for 25 minutes until risen and golden. Place on a wire rack. Gently heat the apricot jam with a splash of water, sieve and brush over the warm loaf to glaze. Mix the icing sugar with enough water to make a thin icing, drizzle over the loaf and sprinkle with the flaked almonds. Leave to cool.

CHRISTMAS BUNS

MAKES 9 / PREP 2–3 hours / BAKE 20–25 minutes

These are rather like sticky Chelsea buns but with a spicy, fruity Christmassy twist. They make a delicious change from shop-bought panettone or even mince pies.

300ml full-fat milk

40g unsalted butter, softened

500g strong white bread flour, plus extra for dusting

10g fine salt

10g instant yeast

1 medium egg, lightly beaten

For the filling

25g unsalted butter, melted

75g soft brown sugar

2 tsp ground cinnamon

100g dried cranberries

100g ready-to-eat dried apricots, chopped

For the glaze

75g apricot jam

For the lemon icing

100g icing sugar

Finely grated zest of ½ lemon

1 tbsp water

1. Warm the milk and butter in a saucepan until the butter melts and the mixture is lukewarm.

2. Tip the flour into a large mixing bowl and add the salt to one side of the bowl and the yeast to the other. Add the milk mixture and the egg and stir together with your hands to make a rough dough. You may need to add a little extra flour.

3. Tip the dough onto a generously floured work surface and begin to knead. Keep kneading for 5–10 minutes. Work through the initial wet stage until the dough starts to form a soft, smooth skin.

4. When your dough feels smooth and silky, put it into a lightly oiled large bowl. Cover with a tea towel and leave to rise until at least doubled in size – at least 1 hour, but it's fine to leave it for 2 or even 3 hours.

5. Line a deep-sided baking tray or roasting dish with baking parchment or silicone paper.

6. Tip the dough out onto a floured surface and, without knocking it back, roll it out to a rectangle about 5mm thick. Tack down the edge closest to you (as this will allow you to pull and tighten the dough as you roll, which gives a nice tight swirl). Brush the surface all over with the melted butter, then sprinkle over the brown sugar, cinnamon and dried fruits. Roll the dough up into a tight cylinder and cut it into 9 slices. Place these, cut side up, in the baking tray or roasting dish, leaving a little space between each slice.

7. Cover the dough with a tea towel and set aside to rise for 30 minutes. Meanwhile, heat your oven to 190°C.

8. Bake the buns for 20–25 minutes, or until risen and golden brown. Warm the apricot jam with a splash of water, sieve and brush over the hot buns to glaze, then set aside to cool on a wire rack.

9. When the buns are cool, mix the ingredients for the lemon icing together to make a smooth icing and trickle across the top of the buns.

SOU
DOU

SOURDOUGH IS BREAD RISEN NATURALLY by airborne yeasts, unlike conventional bread doughs, which rely on manufactured yeast added to the flour by the baker. It is the oldest style of leavened bread, dating back five thousand years, but it is enjoying a renaissance now, and with very good reason. Sourdough bread has real character. With a deep, tangy flavour, robust texture and excellent crust, it's great with cheese, perfect for bruschetta and fabulous for everything from your breakfast toast to crunchy croûtons for salads and soups.

Sourdough baking has become my serious passion. It evokes strong memories for me – of eating wonderful sourdoughs in Italy, France and Cyprus over the years. On Saturdays, I like to go to my bakery when the bakers are off and make these breads on my own. Mixing, kneading and eating them is incredibly satisfying.

Sourdoughs are the pinnacle of bread-making. At first they may seem tricky, but if you master the techniques you will reap the rewards. And you will become a true aficionado of bread!

So, please, do give these recipes a try: they will take you into a whole new area of delicious and deeply satisfying baking.

THE SECRET OF SOURDOUGHS

Creating a sourdough takes longer and is not quite as straightforward as conventional bread-baking. The rising process is much lengthier because natural yeasts work more slowly than commercial yeasts, and the dough tends to become wetter as it rises and proves. The speed at which the dough develops also depends to some extent on the environment and temperature. You have to get a feel for when the dough is ready, but don't be put off. I will help you to judge when a sourdough starter is properly developed, and when a proving loaf is ready for the oven.

Making a sourdough starter is easy. A simple mixture of water, flour and grated apple is enough to activate airborne wild yeasts. This batter-like mixture is the start and needs to be fed once the bubbles of carbon dioxide start to appear. Over a period of a couple of days the mixture will begin to bubble and smell sweet and mildly alcoholic. Leave your starter in an ambient temperature of about 20–24°C. A sheltered spot in your kitchen, away from draughts, is probably the best place, as the temperature is unlikely to drop much below 14°C.

When you come to mix a sourdough, you will find it is invariably softer and slacker than a standard dough. This helps it to rise well. I suggest you start by adding the lower quantity of water suggested in a recipe but, as your confidence grows and you make more loaves, try adding more. You will find the structure of the bread improves.

Even with the lower quantity of water, kneading is very important. Once kneaded properly, a sourdough should not be unmanageably wet or sticky. A 'wet' dough and a 'soft' dough may contain the same amount of water, but the soft one will have been kneaded properly, allowing the gluten to develop and hold the dough together. Knead a sourdough for 5 minutes at the very least, more likely 10 minutes or more. It's quite easy to under-knead a dough but, unless you are using an industrial mixer, it is almost impossible to over-knead one, so don't be afraid to keep going. You are looking for the stage at which the consistency of the dough changes. As the gluten develops, the dough will become smoother, more elastic and more cogent. It will want to hold itself together in a ball, rather than stick to your work surface, and it will develop a soft, smooth skin.

Some of these doughs are very soft, but this way of baking always gives you better results. When shaping the dough, be gentle and take care to avoid ripping it. The use of a proving basket (see page 30) helps to maintain a good shape during proving. Keep it loosely covered with a plastic bag during this stage and the dough will rise. The rising and proving time will vary according to the temperature of your kitchen. If it is around 18°C, expect the dough to take about 12 hours; in a warmer kitchen it is more likely to be 9–10 hours. Don't rush it. Press the dough gently and you will feel the aeration; a bit of resistance is a good indicator that the yeasts are active.

Basic sourdough loaf (see page 132) slowly proving and developing its characteristic flavour.

SOURDOUGH STARTER

PREP 10 minutes

It is important to have an organic apple, free of chemicals, for this, or the starter may not ferment. I like to use a Cox, but any organic apple will do.

1kg strong white bread flour

1 organic apple, grated, with skin, avoiding the core

360ml tepid water

Stage 1:
Mix 500g of the flour with the apple and water ①. Tip this into an airtight container ② and mark the level on the outside of the container (so you can see whether the mix has risen). Cover and leave to ferment for 3 days.

Stage 2:
After 3 days the mix should start to smell quite sweet, a bit like cider. It will be a little darker in colour ③ and will have started to grow; it may also have some bubbles. Check the level against the mark you made on the outside to see how much it has grown. Discard half the mix and add another 250g bread flour and 170ml water – this is called 'feeding'. Mix thoroughly in the bowl. Tip back into the container and leave for a further 2 days.

Stage 3:
There should now be plenty of activity in the dough, indicated by lots of small bubbles ④. If there is nothing happening, look at the side of the container – you'll be able to see whether the dough has risen and fallen by the smearing on the side. If it has risen and fallen, then it is active.

If your starter is active but has sunk down in the tub and a layer of liquid has formed on top, then it is actually over-active. Stir in some more flour to return it to a thick consistency and leave for a day. It should regain the thick, bubbly texture you want. If there is no sign of rising on the container, and no bubbles, leave the dough for a couple more days.

Once your starter is active, discard half of it, as before, and mix in another 250g bread flour and enough water to return it to the consistency of a very wet, sloppy dough. This time leave it for 24 hours. If the starter begins to bubble within this time, then it is ready to use. Ideally, when you come to use it, you want your starter to be thick and bubbly. If you shake it, it should wobble like a jelly, without dropping down. When you put a spoon through it, it should be like a thick batter. If your starter is not bubbling, feed it again, following stage two, and leave it for a further 2 days.

If you are using your starter often, you can leave it at room temperature, feeding it at least every 3 days and whenever you take some to make bread. Simply stir in some strong white bread flour and enough water to return it to the consistency of a very wet dough, bearing in mind that you will need 500g starter for each recipe. Then leave it, covered, until it achieves that thick, bubbly, jelly-like stage. If you are making sourdough less often – say, once a month – then keep the starter, covered, in the fridge. This will slow down the activity and preserve it almost indefinitely, but you must let it come back to room temperature before use. If it seems to be inactive, give it a feed of fresh flour – the bacteria within it are living so they need feeding.

BASIC SOURDOUGH

MAKES 2 loaves / PREP 16–19 hours / BAKE 30–40 minutes

This is a lovely bread to tear and eat with soup or a salad. It also makes great
toast and is an excellent base for bruschetta: cut into generous slices, rub
with a halved clove of garlic and trickle with some very good extra virgin
olive oil before piling on the topping of your choice.

**750g strong white
  bread flour, plus
  extra for dusting**

**500g sourdough
  starter (see page 130)**

15g salt

**350–450ml tepid
  water**

Olive oil for kneading

1. Put the flour, starter and salt into a large mixing bowl. Add 350ml
   water and begin mixing with your hands, adding more water if you
   need to, until you have formed a soft, rough dough and picked up all
   the flour from the sides of the bowl.

2. Coat the work surface with a little olive oil, then tip the dough onto it
   and begin to knead (see page 16). Keep kneading for 5–10 minutes.
   Work through the initial wet stage until the dough starts to form a soft,
   smooth skin (see page 17).

3. When your dough feels smooth and silky, put it into a lightly oiled bowl
   and cover with a tea towel. Leave to rise at 22–24°C (no cooler than 15°C
   and no warmer than 25°C) for 5 hours, or until at least doubled in size.

4. Cover 2 trays with cloths and dust them heavily with flour, or prepare
   2 proving baskets (see page 30).

5. Tip the risen dough onto a lightly floured surface and fold it inwards
   repeatedly until all the air is knocked out and the dough is smooth.
   Divide in half and shape each piece into a smooth ball (see pages 20–1),
   for a cob-shaped loaf.

6. Put each ball of dough on a floured cloth (or in a proving basket) and
   dust with more flour. Put each into a clean plastic bag and leave to prove
   at 22–24°C for 10–13 hours, or until the dough is at least doubled in
   size and springs back when lightly prodded with your finger. If your
   dough has over-proved, it will look wrinkly. This means you will need
   to reshape it (don't knead it) into a ball and leave it to prove again. This
   time it should take 5–6 hours to double in size.

7. When the dough is ready, heat your oven to 200°C. Line 2 baking trays
   with baking parchment or silicone paper.

8. Turn the risen dough upside down so the wrinkled underside is on top
   (this will open up as it bakes). Put the loaves on the prepared baking
   trays and cut a heavy slash across the middle of each.

9. You may need to bake your breads in batches. Put into the oven and
   bake for 30–40 minutes until the loaf is golden brown and sounds
   hollow when tapped on the base. Cool on a wire rack.

BAGUETTE AU LEVAIN

MAKES 5 baguettes / PREP 18 hours / BAKE 25 minutes

'Levain' is another word for a sourdough starter. Baguettes made in this way have a wonderful flavour and a superb crust. There's nothing better with some ripe Brie or Camembert.

750g strong white
   bread flour, plus
   extra for dusting

500g sourdough
   starter (see page 130)

15g salt

350–450ml tepid
   water

Olive oil for kneading

1. Put the flour, starter and salt into a large mixing bowl. Add 350ml water and begin mixing with your hands, adding more water if you need to, until you have formed a soft, rough dough and picked up all the flour from the sides of the bowl.

2. Coat the work surface with a little olive oil, then tip the dough onto it and begin to knead. Keep kneading for 5–10 minutes. Work through the initial wet stage until the dough starts to form a soft, smooth skin.

3. When your dough feels smooth and silky, put it into a lightly oiled bowl and cover with a tea towel. Leave to rise at 22–24°C (no cooler than 15°C and no warmer than 25°C) for 5 hours, or until at least doubled in size.

4. Cover 2 trays with cloths and dust them heavily with flour.

5. Tip the risen dough onto a lightly floured surface and fold it inwards repeatedly until all the air is knocked out and the dough is smooth. Divide it into 5 pieces, each weighing 300g. Shape each piece into a sausage by flattening the dough out slightly and folding the sides into the middle. Then roll up – the top should be smooth with a join running along the length of the base. Then, beginning in the middle, roll out each sausage with your hands. Don't force it out by pressing heavily. Concentrate on the backwards and forwards movement and gently use the weight of your arms to roll out the dough to the length of your oven trays.

6. Put the baguettes, seam side down, on the floured cloths and dust with more flour. Put each tray inside a clean plastic bag and leave to prove at 22–24°C for 12 hours, or until the dough is doubled in size and springs back when lightly prodded with your finger.

7. When the dough is ready, heat your oven to 210°C, and put a roasting tray on the bottom shelf to heat up. Line 2 baking trays with baking parchment or silicone paper.

8. Carefully transfer the baguettes to the prepared baking trays (you should be able to fit three on a tray). Make three long cuts diagonally along the length of each baguette. You may need to bake your breads in batches. Fill the roasting tray with hot water and put the baguettes into the oven. Bake for 25 minutes until golden brown. Cool on a wire rack.

PAIN DE CAMPAGNE

MAKES 2 loaves / PREP 19 hours / BAKE 40 minutes

This traditional French 'country bread', with its measure of rye flour,
is particularly good toasted and topped with a poached egg.

650g strong white
  bread flour, plus
  extra for dusting
100g rye flour
500g sourdough
  starter (see page 130)
15g salt
350–450ml tepid
  water
Olive oil for kneading

1. Put the flours, starter and salt into a large mixing bowl. Add 350ml water and begin mixing with your hands, adding more water if you need to, until you have formed a soft, rough dough and picked up all the flour from the sides of the bowl.

2. Coat the work surface with a little olive oil, then tip the dough onto it and begin to knead. Keep kneading for 5–10 minutes. Work through the initial wet stage until the dough starts to form a soft, smooth skin.

3. When your dough feels smooth and silky, put it into a lightly oiled bowl and cover with a tea towel. Leave to rise at 22–24°C (no cooler than 15°C and no warmer than 25°C) for 5 hours, or until at least doubled in size.

4. Cover 2 trays with cloths and dust them heavily with flour or prepare 2 proving baskets (see page 30).

5. Tip the risen dough onto a lightly floured surface and fold it inwards repeatedly until all the air is knocked out and the dough is smooth. Divide into 2 pieces and shape into ovals (see page 23), tapering the ends of each loaf into points.

6. Put each loaf, seam side down, on a floured cloth (or shape to fit the baskets). Gently rub flour over the top of each loaf. Put inside clean plastic bags and leave to prove at 22–24°C for a minimum of 13 hours, until the dough is at least doubled in size and springs back when lightly prodded with your finger.

7. When the dough is ready, heat your oven to 190°C. Line 2 baking trays with baking parchment or silicone paper.

8. Transfer the loaves to the prepared baking trays. Make a deep cut along the middle of each loaf and then make 2 diagonal slashes on each side; these will open up to form leaf shapes. Bake for 40 minutes until the loaves are well browned and sound hollow when tapped on the base. Cool on a wire rack.

SEEDED SOURDOUGH

MAKES 2 loaves / PREP 20 hours / BAKE 40 minutes

Made with wholemeal flour and packed with seeds, this is a wonderfully tasty and highly nutritious loaf. With all those seeds inside, you will find it takes longer to rise than other sourdoughs and the finished loaf is relatively dense — almost like a rye bread, but delicious nonetheless. It's great for a ploughman's lunch, or sliced thinly and toasted for the cheeseboard.

450g strong white bread flour, plus extra for dusting

350g strong wholemeal bread flour

500g sourdough starter (see page 130)

15g salt

400–500ml tepid water

Olive oil for kneading and oiling the tin

200g pumpkin seeds

200g sunflower seeds

100g poppy seeds

1. Put the flours, starter and salt into a large mixing bowl. Add 400ml water and begin mixing with your hands, adding more water if you need to, until you have formed a soft, rough dough and picked up all the flour from the sides of the bowl.

2. Coat the work surface with a little olive oil, then tip the dough onto it and begin to knead. Keep kneading for 5–10 minutes. Work through the initial wet stage until the dough starts to form a soft, smooth skin.

3. When your dough feels smooth and silky, put it into a lightly oiled bowl and cover with a tea towel. Leave to rise at 22–24°C (no cooler than 15°C and no warmer than 25°C) for 5 hours, or until at least doubled in size.

4. Cover 2 trays with cloths and dust them heavily with flour.

5. Add the pumpkin seeds, sunflower seeds and half the poppy seeds to the dough and knead until well incorporated.

6. Tip the risen dough onto a lightly floured surface, divide it in half and shape each piece into a sausage. Scatter the remaining poppy seeds on a clean surface and roll each loaf in the seeds to coat. Place, seam side down, on the floured cloths.

7. Put each tray inside a clean plastic bag. Leave to prove at 22–24°C for 14 hours, or until the dough is at least doubled in size and springs back when lightly prodded with your finger.

8. When the dough is ready, heat your oven to 190°C. Line 2 baking trays with baking parchment or silicone paper.

9. Transfer each loaf to a prepared baking tray. Snip deeply into the top of the loaves along their length with scissors. Bake for 40 minutes or until the bread sounds hollow when tapped on the base. Cool on a wire rack.

SPITFIRE SOURDOUGH

MAKES 2 loaves / PREP 18 hours / BAKE 40 minutes

I love the deep, tangy flavour of this bread — it's just fantastic with cheese
and another glass of beer! You don't have to use Spitfire, any good ale will do.

**750g strong white
bread flour, plus
extra for dusting**

**500g sourdough
starter (see page 130)**

15g salt

**250ml good-quality
ale, such as Spitfire**

**100–200ml tepid
water**

Olive oil for kneading

For the beer paste

**125ml good-quality
ale, such as Spitfire**

100g rye flour

1. Put the flour, starter and salt into a large mixing bowl. Add the beer
   and about 100ml water and begin mixing with your hands, adding more
   water if you need to, until you have formed a soft, rough dough and
   picked up all the flour from the sides of the bowl.

2. Coat the work surface with a little olive oil, then tip the dough onto it
   and begin to knead. Keep kneading for 5–10 minutes. Work through
   the initial wet stage until the dough starts to form a soft, smooth skin.

3. When your dough feels smooth and silky, put it into a lightly oiled bowl
   and cover with a tea towel. Leave to rise at 22–24°C (no cooler than 15°C
   and no warmer than 25°C) for 5 hours, or until at least doubled in size.

4. Cover 2 trays with cloths and dust them heavily with flour or prepare
   2 proving baskets (see page 30).

5. Tip the risen dough onto a lightly floured surface and fold it inwards
   repeatedly until all the air is knocked out and the dough is smooth.
   Divide the risen dough in half and shape each piece into a round,
   smooth ball (see pages 20–1), for a cob-shaped loaf.

6. Put each ball of dough on a floured cloth (or in a basket) and put inside
   a clean plastic bag. Leave to prove at 22–24°C for 12 hours, or until the
   dough is at least doubled in size and springs back when lightly prodded
   with your finger.

7. About an hour before you think the loaves will be ready, mix the beer
   and rye flour together with a whisk to make a paste and leave to stand for
   an hour.

8. When the dough is ready, heat your oven to 190°C. Line 2 baking trays
   with baking parchment or silicone paper.

9. Transfer the loaves to the prepared baking trays. Smear the beer paste
   all over the top of each one, then slash a deep crosshatch pattern on top.
   Bake for 40 minutes or until the loaves sound hollow when tapped on
   the base. Cool on a wire rack.

WALNUT SOURDOUGH

MAKES 2 loaves / PREP 20 hours / BAKE 40 minutes

Walnuts are an obvious choice for inclusion in a sourdough. Their flavour echoes and enhances that of the bread and they give this loaf a wonderful texture too.

750g strong white
   bread flour, plus
   extra for dusting
500g sourdough
   starter (see page 130)
300g walnut pieces
15g salt
350–450ml tepid
   water
Olive oil for kneading

1. Put the flour, starter, walnuts and salt into a large mixing bowl. Add 350ml water and begin mixing with your hands, adding more water if you need to, until you have formed a soft, rough dough and picked up all the flour from the sides of the bowl.

2. Coat the work surface with a little olive oil, then tip the dough onto it and begin to knead. Keep kneading for 5–10 minutes. Work through the initial wet stage until the dough starts to form a soft, smooth skin.

3. When your dough feels smooth and silky, put it into a lightly oiled bowl and cover with a tea towel. Leave to rise at 22–24°C (no cooler than 15°C and no warmer than 25°C) for 5 hours, or until at least doubled in size.

4. Cover 2 trays with cloths and dust them heavily with flour or prepare 2 proving baskets (see page 30).

5. Tip the risen dough onto a lightly floured work surface and fold it repeatedly in on itself until all the air is knocked out. Divide the dough into 2 pieces. Flatten each piece out and then roll it up into a sausage. Roll out each sausage until about 25cm long.

6. Place each loaf, seam side down, on a floured cloth (or shape to fit the baskets). Put each inside a clean plastic bag. Leave to prove at 22–24°C for 14 hours, or until the dough is doubled in size and springs back when lightly prodded with your finger.

7. When the dough is ready, heat your oven to 190°C. Line 2 baking trays with baking parchment or silicone paper.

8. Transfer each loaf to a prepared baking tray. Gently rub flour onto the surface of each loaf. Using a pair of scissors, make cuts all over the loaves in a criss-cross pattern. Bake for 40 minutes or until the loaves sound hollow when tapped on the base. Cool on a wire rack.

SOUR OLIVE BREAD

MAKES 2 loaves / PREP 18 hours / BAKE 40 minutes

Olives and coriander is a favourite combination of mine, as you will have discovered if you've made the delicious Cypriot-style loaf on page 99. This sourdough is a deeply flavoursome loaf, which is wonderful simply toasted and drizzled with olive oil.

750g strong white bread flour, plus extra for dusting

500g sourdough starter (see page 130)

15g salt

300–400ml tepid water

Olive oil for kneading

200g good-quality black olives, pitted but whole

100g good-quality green olives, pitted but whole

A large bunch of coriander (about 100g), stalks removed, roughly chopped

1. Put the flour, starter and salt into a large bowl. Add 300ml water and begin mixing with your hands, adding more water if you need to, until you have formed a soft, rough dough and picked up all the flour from the sides of the bowl.

2. Coat the work surface with a little olive oil, then tip the dough onto it and begin to knead. Keep kneading for 5–10 minutes. Work through the initial wet stage until the dough starts to form a soft, smooth skin.

3. When your dough feels smooth and silky, put it into a lightly oiled bowl and cover with a tea towel. Leave to rise at 22–24°C (no cooler than 15°C and no warmer than 25°C) for 5 hours, or until at least doubled in size.

4. Cover 2 trays with cloths and dust them heavily with flour or prepare 2 proving baskets (see page 30).

5. Add all the olives and the coriander to the dough and knead them in by hand for several minutes until they are well dispersed.

6. Tip the risen dough onto a lightly floured surface and fold it in on itself a few times to knock out all the air. Divide the dough into 2 pieces and shape into ovals (see page 23).

7. Place each loaf, seam side down, on a floured cloth (or shape to fit the baskets). Gently rub flour all over the top of each loaf and put each inside a clean plastic bag. Leave to prove at 22–24°C for 12 hours, or until the dough is doubled in size and springs back if lightly prodded with your finger.

8. When the dough is ready, heat your oven to 190°C. Line 2 baking trays with baking parchment or silicone paper.

9. Transfer the loaves to the prepared baking trays and make a deep cut down the middle of each one. Bake for 40 minutes. The bread is ready when it sounds hollow if you tap it on the base. Cool on a wire rack.

CHEDDAR AND APPLE SOURDOUGH

MAKES 2 loaves / PREP 19 hours / BAKE 35 minutes

This bread, I'm proud to say, has graced the food hall of Harrods. A slice
or two is gorgeous served with a big bowl of salad or some soup.

**750g strong white
bread flour, plus
extra for dusting**

**500g sourdough
starter (see page 130)**

15g salt

**350–450ml tepid
water**

Olive oil for kneading

For the filling

200g Cheddar, grated

**3 dessert apples, cored
and roughly chopped**

To finish

50g Cheddar, grated

1. Put the flour, starter and salt into a large bowl. Add 350ml water and begin mixing with your hands, adding more water if you need to, until you have formed a soft, rough dough and picked up all the flour from the sides of the bowl.

2. Coat the work surface with a little olive oil, then tip the dough onto it and begin to knead. Keep kneading for 5–10 minutes. Work through the initial wet stage until the dough starts to form a soft, smooth skin.

3. When your dough feels smooth and silky, put it into a lightly oiled bowl and cover with a tea towel. Leave to rise at 22–24°C (no cooler than 15°C and no warmer than 25°C) for 5 hours, or until at least doubled in size.

4. Cover 2 trays with cloths and dust them heavily with flour.

5. Tip the risen dough onto a lightly floured work surface and fold it in on itself a few times to knock out all the air. Divide the dough into 2 pieces. Flatten each piece out into a rough rectangle, about 30 x 20cm and 1–2cm deep. Sprinkle half the grated Cheddar over one side of each rectangle and top with half of the apples, leaving a 1cm clear margin along the edges. Fold the dough over to make a smaller rectangle and press the edges down firmly to seal.

6. Put each loaf on a floured cloth and place inside a clean plastic bag. Leave to prove at 22–24°C for 13 hours, or until the dough is doubled in size and springs back when lightly prodded with your finger.

7. When the dough is ready, heat your oven to 200°C. Line 2 baking trays with baking parchment or silicone paper.

8. Transfer the loaves to the prepared baking trays. Sprinkle the top of each loaf with grated Cheddar and make a deep indentation along each loaf with your finger. Bake for 35 minutes, until the loaves sound hollow when tapped on the base. Cool on a wire rack.

SMOKED BACON AND GARLIC SOURDOUGH

MAKES 2 loaves / PREP 15 hours / BAKE 35 minutes

This bread has a deeply savoury flavour and goes brilliantly with char-grilled meat and vegetables. Try splitting the loaf lengthways and placing it on the barbecue or griddle cut-side down for a couple of minutes before serving.

750g strong white
   bread flour, plus
   extra for dusting
500g sourdough
   starter (see page 130)
15g salt
350–450ml tepid
   water
Olive oil for kneading

For the filling
3 large garlic bulbs
A little olive oil
200g smoked bacon

1. Put the flour, starter and salt into a large mixing bowl. Add 350ml water and begin mixing with your hands, adding more water if you need to, until you have formed a soft, rough dough and picked up all the flour from the sides of the bowl.

2. Coat the work surface with a little olive oil, then tip the dough onto it and begin to knead. Keep kneading for 5–10 minutes. Work through the initial wet stage until the dough starts to form a soft, smooth skin.

3. When your dough feels smooth and silky, put it into a lightly oiled bowl and cover with a tea towel. Leave to rise at 22–24˚C (no cooler than 15˚C and no warmer than 25˚C) for 5 hours, or until at least doubled in size.

4. Meanwhile, heat your oven to 190˚C. Slice the very top off each garlic bulb, to just expose the cloves inside. Put onto a piece of foil and trickle with a little olive oil. Scrunch up the foil around the garlic in a loose parcel. Roast for about 45 minutes, until the cloves are very tender. When cool enough to handle, separate and squeeze the soft garlic cloves out of their skins into a bowl. Mash them to a rough purée using a fork. Heat a little olive oil in a frying pan, add the bacon and cook gently on both sides until tender. Remove and set aside to cool, then chop.

5. Cover 2 trays with cloths and dust them heavily with flour or prepare 2 proving baskets (see page 30).

6. Tip the risen dough onto a lightly floured surface. Fold it inwards repeatedly until all the air is knocked out and the dough is smooth. Divide into 2 pieces. Flatten out each piece and spread with half the garlic purée, then sprinkle over half the bacon. Roll up the dough to sandwich the filling inside, then shape into 2 ovals (see page 23).

7. Place each loaf on a floured cloth (or in a basket) and put inside a clean plastic bag. Leave to prove at 22–24˚C for 9 hours, or until the dough is at least doubled in size and springs back when lightly prodded with your finger.

8. When the dough is ready, heat your oven to 200˚C. Line 2 baking trays with baking parchment or silicone paper.

9. Transfer the loaves to the prepared baking trays, sprinkle with water and gently rub with flour. Bake for 35 minutes or until the loaves sound hollow when tapped on the base. Cool on a wire rack.

SOURDOUGH FILLED WITH EPOISSE CHEESE

MAKES 2 loaves / PREP 15 hours / BAKE 40 minutes

Epoisse is a rich, creamy, washed-rind cheese with a pungent aroma.
It really holds its own with the tangy flavour of sourdough, making
this a sumptuous, rich loaf.

750g strong white bread flour, plus extra for dusting

500g sourdough starter (see page 130)

15g salt

350–450ml tepid water

Olive oil for kneading

For the filling

300g ripe Epoisse cheese

150g flaked almonds, toasted

1. Put the flour, starter and salt into a large mixing bowl. Add 350ml water and begin mixing with your hands, adding more water if you need to, until you have formed a soft, rough dough and picked up all the flour from the sides of the bowl.

2. Coat the work surface with a little olive oil, then tip the dough onto it and begin to knead. Keep kneading for 5–10 minutes. Work through the initial wet stage until the dough starts to form a soft, smooth skin.

3. When your dough feels smooth and silky, put it into a lightly oiled bowl and cover with a tea towel. Leave to rise at 22–24°C (no cooler than 15°C and no warmer than 25°C) for 5 hours, or until at least doubled in size.

4. Cover 2 trays with cloths and dust them heavily with flour or prepare 2 proving baskets (see page 30).

5. Tip the risen dough onto a lightly floured surface. Fold it inwards repeatedly until all the air is knocked out and the dough is smooth. Divide into 2 pieces. Flatten each piece out using your hands and put half of the Epoisse on top. If it is ripe, you should easily be able to spread it over the dough. If it's a bit firm, you can break it up into chunks first. Sprinkle half the toasted flaked almonds on each piece. Roll up the dough to sandwich the filling inside.

6. Now you need to shape the dough into a ball (see pages 20–1). Begin tucking the dough underneath itself, using both hands, turning the dough continually until the dough on the top of the ball becomes tight. The more you tuck and turn the dough, the tighter it will get.

7. Place each ball of dough, smooth side down, on a floured cloth (or in a basket). Put each inside a clean plastic bag. Leave to prove at 22–24°C for 9 hours, or until the dough is doubled in size and springs back when lightly prodded with your finger.

8. When the dough is ready, heat your oven to 190°C. Line 2 baking trays with baking parchment or silicone paper.

9. Tip each loaf carefully onto a prepared baking tray. Bake for 40 minutes or until the bread sounds hollow when tapped on the base. Cool on a wire rack.

ROSEMARY AND LEMON SOURDOUGH

MAKES 2 loaves / PREP 15 hours / BAKE 30 minutes

Rosemary and lemon combine to give this focaccia-style sourdough a lovely flavour. This is a great bread to eat with hearty soups and stews.

750g strong white bread flour, plus extra for dusting

500g sourdough starter (see page 130)

15g salt

2 tbsp chopped fresh rosemary

Finely grated zest of 2 lemons

350–450ml tepid water

Olive oil for kneading and to finish

To finish

Flaky sea salt

Chopped fresh rosemary

1. Put the flour, starter, salt, rosemary and lemon zest into a large mixing bowl. Add 350ml water and begin mixing with your hands, adding more water if you need to, until you have formed a soft, rough dough and picked up all the flour from the sides of the bowl.

2. Coat the work surface with a little olive oil, then tip the dough onto it and begin to knead. Keep kneading for 5–10 minutes. Work through the initial wet stage until the dough starts to form a soft, smooth skin.

3. When your dough feels smooth and silky, put it into a lightly oiled bowl and cover with a tea towel. Leave to rise at 22–24°C (no cooler than 15°C and no warmer than 25°C) for 5 hours, or until at least doubled in size.

4. Rub 2 baking tins, each about 33 x 23cm, with a little olive oil.

5. Tip the risen dough onto a lightly floured work surface. Fold it inwards repeatedly until all the air is knocked out and the dough is smooth. Divide into 2 pieces. Roll out each piece to fit the dimensions of your baking tins and transfer the dough to them.

6. Cover each tin with a clean plastic bag. Leave to prove at 22–24°C for 9 hours, or until the dough is doubled in size and springs back when lightly prodded with your finger.

7. When the dough is ready, heat your oven to 200°C.

8. Use your fingers to make deep indentations all over the top of the dough. Drizzle with olive oil and sprinkle with sea salt and rosemary. Bake for 30 minutes or until golden brown. Cool on a wire rack.

MUESLI AND BANANA SOURDOUGH

MAKES 2 loaves / PREP 19 hours / BAKE 40 minutes

This is a tried-and-tested favourite of mine: a bread I often used to make when I was working in hotel kitchens, to be served at breakfast. It always went down very well.

750g strong white
    bread flour, plus
    extra for dusting
500g sourdough
    starter (see page 130)
15g salt
3 bananas, peeled and
    broken into pieces
300g of your favourite
    muesli mix
350–450ml tepid
    water
Olive oil for kneading
50g rolled oats
    for topping

1. Put the flour, starter, salt, bananas and muesli into a large mixing bowl. Add 350ml water and begin mixing with your hands, adding more water if you need to, until you have formed a soft, rough dough and picked up all the flour from the sides of the bowl (the bananas will break down as you work).

2. Coat the work surface with a little olive oil, then tip the dough onto it and begin to knead. Keep kneading for 5–10 minutes. Work through the initial wet stage until the dough starts to form a soft, smooth skin.

3. When your dough feels smooth and silky, put it into a lightly oiled bowl and cover with a tea towel. Leave to rise at 22–24°C (no cooler than 15°C and no warmer than 25°C) for 5 hours, or until at least doubled in size.

4. Cover 2 trays with cloths and dust them heavily with flour or prepare 2 proving baskets (see page 30).

5. Tip the risen dough onto a lightly floured work surface. Fold it inwards repeatedly until all the air is knocked out and the dough is smooth. Divide into 2 pieces and shape each piece into a round, smooth ball (see pages 20–1), as for a cob.

6. Place each loaf on a floured cloth (or in a basket) and put inside a clean plastic bag. Leave to prove at 22–24°C for 13 hours, or until the dough is doubled in size and springs back if lightly prodded with your finger.

7. When the dough is ready, heat your oven to 200°C. Line 2 baking trays with baking parchment or silicone paper.

8. Transfer the loaves to the prepared baking trays. Brush the top of each loaf with a little water and sprinkle on the rolled oats. Then, using a plastic scraper, mark each loaf into 8 pieces, pressing all the way down to the baking tray. Bake for 40 minutes or until the loaves sound hollow when tapped on the base. Cool on a wire rack.

CHOCOLATE AND APRICOT SOURDOUGH

MAKES 2 loaves / PREP 19 hours / BAKE 35 minutes

The combination of dark chocolate and dried apricots is particularly good in this breakfast or teatime bread. As the chocolate bakes, it takes on a lovely malty taste. You can substitute morello cherries (from a tin or jar) for the apricots if you like, but use only 200g and drain them well first.

750g strong white bread flour, plus extra for dusting

500g sourdough starter (see page 130)

15g salt

250g dark chocolate nibs (or chopped dark chocolate)

300g organic dried apricots, chopped

350–450ml tepid water

Olive oil for kneading

1. Put the flour, starter, salt, chocolate and apricots into a large mixing bowl. Add 350ml water and begin mixing with your hands, adding more water if you need to, until you have formed a soft, rough dough and picked up all the flour from the sides of the bowl.

2. Coat the work surface with a little olive oil, then tip the dough onto it and begin to knead. Keep kneading for 5–10 minutes. Work through the initial wet stage until the dough starts to form a soft, smooth skin.

3. When your dough feels smooth and silky, put it into a lightly oiled bowl and cover with a tea towel. Leave to rise at 22–24°C (no cooler than 15°C and no warmer than 25°C) for 5 hours, or until at least doubled in size.

4. Cover 2 trays with cloths and dust them heavily with flour or prepare 2 proving baskets (see page 30).

5. Tip the risen dough onto a lightly floured work surface. Fold it inwards repeatedly until all the air is knocked out and the dough is smooth. Divide into 2 pieces and shape each piece into a round, smooth ball (see pages 20–1), as for a cob.

6. Place each loaf on a floured cloth (or in a basket) and put inside a clean plastic bag. Leave to prove at 22–24°C for 13 hours, or until the dough is doubled in size and springs back if lightly prodded with your finger.

7. When the dough is ready, heat your oven to 200°C. Line 2 baking trays with baking parchment or silicone paper.

8. Transfer each loaf to a prepared baking tray. Flour the top of each loaf, rubbing it gently into the skin. Cut 4 or 5 lines across the top of each loaf, then turn the trays 90° and repeat, cutting across the first line of cuts to make a diamond pattern. Bake for 35 minutes or until the loaves sound hollow when tapped on the base. Cool on a wire rack.

LAVENDER HONEY AND TOASTED ALMOND SOURDOUGH

MAKES 2 loaves / PREP 15 hours / BAKE 35 minutes

This bread is strongly influenced by my visits to the Loire Valley in France, famed for its fields of lavender, which lends its fragrance delectably to honey. But don't be put off from making this bread if you only have ordinary honey, it will still be really delicious.

750g strong white bread flour, plus extra for dusting

500g sourdough starter (see page 130)

15g salt

350–450ml tepid water

100g lavender honey

225g flaked almonds, toasted

Olive oil for kneading

1. Put the flour, starter and salt into a large mixing bowl. Add 350ml water and begin mixing with your hands, adding more water if you need to, until you have formed a soft, rough dough and picked up all the flour from the sides of the bowl.

2. Coat the work surface with a little olive oil, then tip the dough onto it and begin to knead. Keep kneading for 5–10 minutes. Work through the initial wet stage until the dough starts to form a soft, smooth skin.

3. When your dough feels smooth and silky, put it into a lightly oiled bowl and cover with a tea towel. Leave to rise at 22–24°C (no cooler than 15°C and no warmer than 25°C) for 5 hours, or until at least doubled in size.

4. Cover 2 trays with cloths and dust them heavily with flour.

5. Tip the risen dough onto a lightly floured work surface. Fold it inwards repeatedly until all the air is knocked out and the dough is smooth. Divide into 2 pieces. Press each piece out into a rough rectangle and spread with half the honey, then scatter with one-third of the almonds. Roll up each rectangle into a sausage, then roll each sausage until about 22cm long. Taper the ends by rolling with the edges of your hands.

6. Scatter the remaining almonds on a clean surface. Rub a little water on each loaf and then roll the loaf in the almonds to coat.

7. Place a loaf on each tray and put inside a clean plastic bag. Leave to prove at 22–24°C for 9 hours, or until the dough is at least doubled in size and springs back when lightly prodded with your finger.

8. When the dough is ready, heat your oven to 190°C. Line 2 baking trays with baking parchment or silicone paper.

9. Put a loaf on each prepared baking tray. Bake for 35 minutes or until the loaves sound hollow when tapped on the base. Cool on a wire rack.

CROISS

DA

BR

IF YOU HAVE EVER GAZED at the display in your favourite patisserie and wished you could recreate those delicious pastries at home, then this is the chapter for you. The recipes use sweetened yeasted doughs and lots of butter to produce those classic baked goods that you might have thought were the sole preserve of professional bakers.

Making these rich doughs takes time, to achieve the layering of the butter and dough that gives the pastries their characteristic flakiness and charm. However, most of this time is resting and proving; the hands-on work is relatively brief.

The recipes that follow are quite challenging, but the results are fantastic. I promise you that the homemade croissant you eat warm from your oven will be the best you have ever tasted. And, once you've mastered the techniques, there are countless ways to use these doughs.

A word of advice: choose your ingredients carefully, opting for the best you can find. It will make all the difference.

ANTS,

NISH &

OCHE

MASTERING ENRICHED DOUGHS

Making pastries such as croissants and Danish, where butter is layered inside the dough, or 'laminated', is all about temperature. Once you get to grips with that, you are on the right track. Keeping everything cold means the butter stays in firm, discrete layers, trapped within the dough, and makes the dough itself easier to handle. If the dough gets warm and the butter starts to soften, it will pour out during baking and the pastry will be bread-like rather than flaky. For the same reason, you cannot rise and prove your croissants or Danish in a warm place or the butter will soften too much.

Temperature is crucial when making brioche too: the butter needs to be very soft when added, so that it can be easily incorporated, but then the dough must be chilled in order for it to become firm enough to shape.

The recipes in this chapter produce relatively large numbers of pastries. If you don't want to bake them all at once, you can freeze the pastries before proving. Wrap the formed croissants or Danish pastries in cling film and store them in a container in the freezer. They can be kept frozen for up to 6 months and then just need to be defrosted and proved before baking. Bring them out of the freezer the night before you want them. If, for example, you want freshly baked croissants for breakfast, bring them out of the freezer at about 11pm and put them on a baking tray lined with baking parchment. Cover with a plastic bag and then in the morning, somewhere between 7am and 9am, brush them with beaten egg and bake them in your preheated oven.

A NOTE ON INGREDIENTS

When making doughs for croissants, Danish and brioche, use a good strong white bread flour, which is high in gluten. This will give you the elastic, flexible dough required for these pastries.

The type of butter you use is also important. I always choose an unsalted Normandy butter. This is a very pure butter with a higher melting point than other unsalted butters, so it remains firm for longer while you are handling it, and it is less likely to leak from the pastry during baking. I also happen to think it tastes fantastic.

If you are using fruit, in a Danish pastry for example, get it as fresh as possible. Do not use under-ripe fruit as the flavour will be disappointing. In most of my Danish recipes, you can replace the suggested fruit with another of your choice.

Shaping classic Danish pastries (see Raspberry Danish, page 181).

CROISSANTS

MAKES 12 / PREP 16–17 hours, including overnight chilling / BAKE 15–20 minutes

Croissants are ubiquitous these days and they can be very disappointing. But, made well, there is nothing better than a warm croissant. Just add coffee and a newspaper for the perfect breakfast. Making the dough is a long process, but the technique itself is relatively easy, particularly if you follow the sequence of step-by-step photographs over the page. The crucial thing is neatness when adding the rolled-out butter. If the butter does not fit neatly right to the edge of the dough, you will end up with parts of the croissant with no butter. It's also important to keep everything cool as you work, including your hands.

500g strong white bread flour, plus extra for dusting

10g salt, plus a pinch for the eggwash

80g caster sugar

10g instant yeast

300ml cool water

300g chilled unsalted butter, preferably a good-quality Normandy butter

1 medium egg to glaze

1. Put the flour into the bowl of a mixer fitted with a dough hook. Add the salt and sugar to one side of the bowl and the yeast to the other. Add the water and mix on a slow speed for 2 minutes, then on a medium speed for 6 minutes. The dough should be fairly stiff.

2. Tip the dough out onto a lightly floured surface and shape it into a ball. Dust with flour, put into a clean plastic bag and chill in the fridge for an hour.

3. On a lightly floured surface, roll out your dough to a rectangle ①, about 60 x 20cm; it should be about 1cm thick. Flatten the butter to a rectangle ②, about 40 x 19cm, by bashing it with a rolling pin. Put the butter on the dough so that it covers the bottom two-thirds of the dough ③. Make sure that it is positioned neatly and comes almost to the edges.

4. Fold the exposed dough at the top down over one-third of the butter ④. Now gently cut off the exposed bit of butter, without going through the dough, and put it on top of the dough you have just folded down ⑤. Fold the bottom half of the dough up ⑥. You will now have a sandwich of two layers of butter and three of dough. Pinch the edges lightly to seal in the butter ⑦. Put the dough back into the plastic bag and chill in the fridge for an hour to harden the butter.

5. Take the dough out of the bag and put it on the lightly floured work surface with the short end towards you ⑧. Roll into a rectangle, about 60 x 20cm, as before ⑨. This time fold up one-third of the dough ⑩ and then fold the top third down on top ⑪ to make a neat square ⑫. This is called a single turn. Put the dough back into the plastic bag ⑬ and chill for another hour. Repeat this stage twice more, putting the dough back into the fridge for an hour between turns.

6. Your dough now needs to be left in the fridge for 8 hours, or overnight, to rest and rise slightly.

7. When you are ready to shape the croissants, line 2 or 3 baking trays with baking parchment or silicone paper.

8. Put the dough onto a lightly floured surface and roll out to a rectangle, a little more than 42cm long and 30cm wide (14); it should be about 7mm thick. Trim the edges to neaten them.

9. Cut the rectangle lengthways into 2 strips, then cut triangles along the length of each strip (15); these should be 12cm wide at the base and about 15cm high (from the middle of the base to the tip). Once you have cut the first triangle, you can use it as a template for the rest. You should get 6 triangles from each strip.

10. Before rolling, hold down the wide base of the triangle and gently tug the opposite thin end to cause a slight tension in the dough (16). Now starting at the thick end of each triangle, roll it up into a croissant (17). You will have 12 medium-sized croissants (18). For a traditional crescent shape, turn the ends in towards each other slightly.

11. Put the croissants on the prepared baking trays, leaving space in between for them to expand; allow 4–6 per tray. Put each tray inside a clean plastic bag and leave the croissants to rise at cool room temperature (18–24°C) until at least doubled in size. This should take about 2 hours.

12. Heat your oven to 200°C.

13. Lightly whisk the egg with a pinch of salt to make an egg wash. Brush the top and sides of the croissants with the eggwash. Bake for 15–20 minutes or until golden brown. Cool on a wire rack. Eat warm.

BACON AND CHEESE CROISSANTS

Combine 200g chopped cooked back bacon with 150g grated Cheddar. Cut out the triangles of croissant dough, as above, then put a tablespoonful of the bacon and cheese mix at the thick end of each triangle. Roll up into croissants, as above. Place on lined baking trays, put inside clean plastic bags and leave to prove, as above, for about 2 hours, until at least doubled in size. Brush with eggwash, as above, and bake at 200°C for 15–20 minutes. Serve the croissants warm (not hot as the cheese will be very hot when they come out of the oven) for breakfast or brunch.

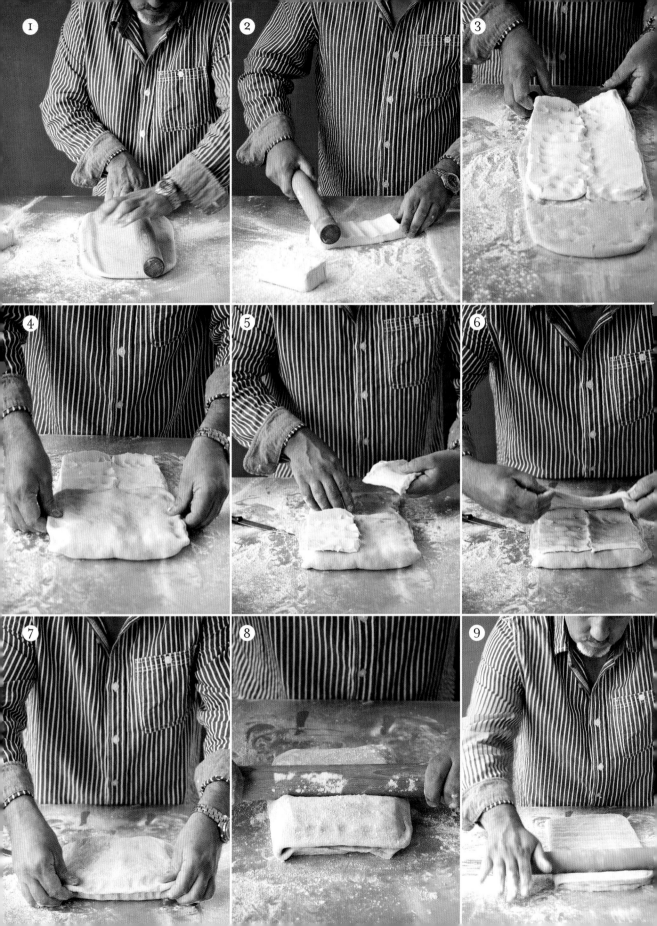

ALMOND CROISSANTS

MAKES 12 / PREP 3 hours / BAKE 15–20 minutes

I have been making these luxurious pastries for years and still find them totally
irresistible. The blend of soft, almondy frangîpane in a light, flaky, buttery
pastry is unbeatable.

**1 quantity croissant
   dough (see page
   164), chilled**
1 medium egg to glaze
Pinch of salt

For the filling and topping
**1 quantity frangîpane
   (see page 174)**
50g flaked almonds

1. Line 2 or 3 baking trays with baking parchment or silicone paper.

2. Roll out the rested croissant dough and cut into triangles (as described
   on page 165), then spread about 1 tbsp of frangîpane from the thick end
   to the point of each triangle (1) and roll up into a croissant shape (2).

3. Put the croissants on the prepared baking trays, leaving space in between
   for them to expand; allow 4–6 per tray. Put each tray inside a clean
   plastic bag and leave the croissants to rise at cool room temperature
   (18–24°C) until at least doubled in size. This should take about 2 hours.

4. Heat your oven to 200°C.

5. Lightly whisk the egg with a pinch of salt to make an egg wash. Brush
   the top and sides of the croissants with the eggwash and sprinkle the top
   with flaked almonds. Bake for 15–20 minutes or until golden brown.
   Cool on a wire rack. Eat at room temperature, or slightly warm.

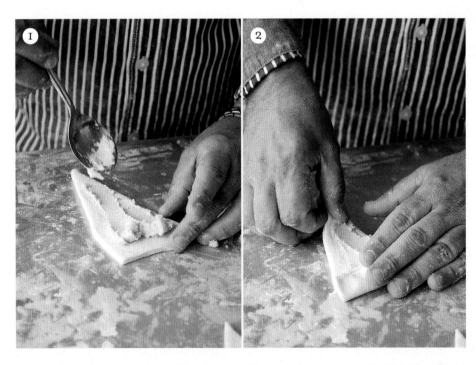

PAIN AU CHOCOLAT

MAKES 12 / PREP 3 hours / BAKE 15–20 minutes

You can fill these lovely pastries with the chocolate of your choice. A finger of dark chocolate is traditional but you could use milk chocolate, orange chocolate or, if you are feeling very wicked, Mars Bars cut into fingers.

1 quantity croissant dough (see page 164), chilled

2 medium eggs, lightly beaten with a splash of milk

225g chocolate of your choice (see above), cut into fingers

1. Line 2 or 3 baking trays with baking parchment or silicone paper.

2. Roll out the rested croissant dough and cut into triangles (as described on page 165), then lay a finger of chocolate across the thick end of each triangle and roll up into a croissant shape.

3. Put the pain au chocolat on the prepared baking trays, with the join underneath, leaving space in between for them to expand; allow 4–6 per tray. Press down firmly on each pain au chocolat; this will prevent them from bursting at the seam.

4. Put each tray inside a clean plastic bag and leave the pastries to rise at cool room temperature (18–24°C) until at least doubled in size. This should take about 2 hours.

5. Heat your oven to 200°C.

6. When the pain au chocolat are ready, brush each one with the beaten egg and milk and bake for 15–20 minutes or until browned and puffed. Cool on a wire rack. Eat at room temperature, or slightly warm.

DANISH PASTRY DOUGH

MAKES I.Ikg: about 25 pastries / PREP 14 hours, including overnight chilling

This is my favourite pastry dough. It's extremely versatile and can be used
to make a variety of delicious 'morning goods', from apple turnovers to
strawberry- and cream-filled pastries. It's easy to shape in different ways
too. As for croissant dough, well-chilled, good-quality butter is essential
(see page 162). Neatness when folding is also imperative. The rolling and
folding technique is the same as the one used for croissants, so refer to the
photographs on page 166, as indicated below.

500g strong white
   bread flour, plus
   extra for dusting
10g salt
80g caster sugar
10g instant yeast
2 medium eggs
90ml cool water
125ml tepid full-fat
   milk
250g chilled unsalted
   butter, preferably
   a good-quality
   Normandy butter

1. Put the flour into the bowl of a mixer fitted with a dough hook. Add
   the salt and sugar to one side of the bowl and the yeast to the other. Add
   the eggs, water and milk and mix on a slow speed for 2 minutes, then on
   a medium speed for 6 minutes.

2. Tip the dough out onto a lightly floured surface and shape it into a ball.
   Dust with flour, put into a clean plastic bag and chill in the fridge for
   an hour.

3. On a lightly floured surface, roll out your chilled dough to a rectangle,
   about 50 x 20cm and about 1cm thick (1) page 166. Flatten the butter
   to a rectangle (2), about 33 x 19cm, by bashing it with a rolling pin. Lay
   the butter on the dough so that it covers the bottom two-thirds of it (3).
   Make sure that it is positioned neatly and comes almost to the edges.

4. Fold the exposed dough at the top down over one-third of the butter (4).
   Now gently cut off the exposed bit of butter, without going through the
   dough, and put it on top of the dough you have just folded down (5).
   Fold the bottom half of the dough up (6). You will now have a sandwich
   of two layers of butter and three of dough. Pinch the edges lightly to seal
   in the butter (7). Put the dough back in the plastic bag and chill for an
   hour to harden the butter.

5. Take the dough out of the bag and put it on the lightly floured surface
   with the short end towards you (8). Now roll it out to a rectangle, about
   50 x 20cm, as before (9). This time fold up one-third of the dough (10)
   and then fold the top third down on top (11). This is called a single turn.
   Put the dough back in the plastic bag and chill for another hour. Repeat
   this stage twice more, putting the dough back into the fridge for an hour
   between turns.

6. Your dough now needs to be left in the fridge for 8 hours, or overnight,
   to rest and rise slightly. It is then ready to use.

FRANGIPANE

MAKES about 400g / PREP 10 minutes

Use this lovely, fragrant almondy paste in almond croissants (see page 169)
or Danish almond pastries (see page 178).

100g unsalted butter, softened

45g caster sugar

2 large eggs

75g plain flour

½ tsp baking powder

100g ground almonds

I tsp almond extract

1. Put the butter and sugar into the bowl of a mixer fitted with a paddle and mix for 3 minutes (or do this with a hand-held electric whisk). Add the eggs and a good tablespoonful of the flour and mix for a further 2 minutes.

2. Now add the remaining flour, baking powder, ground almonds and almond extract. Mix for another 2 minutes. The frangipane is now ready for use. Alternatively, it can be chilled until needed, which will make it easier to shape.

CREME PATISSIERE

MAKES about 750ml / PREP 20 minutes

This classic sweet, thick custard is an essential component of many cakes and pastries, such as raspberry, blueberry and apricot Danish pastries (see page 181) and apple brioche (see page 189), and is a great thing to have in your repertoire.

100g caster sugar

4 medium egg yolks

40g cornflour

500ml full-fat milk

2 vanilla pods

40g butter

1. Whisk the sugar, egg yolks and cornflour together in a bowl until smoothly combined, and set aside.

2. Pour the milk into a large, heavy-based pan. Split the vanilla pods open, scrape out the seeds with the tip of a knife and add these to the milk with the empty pods. Bring to the boil, then remove from the heat.

3. Pour about a quarter of the hot milk onto the egg mixture and whisk together. Then return this mixture to the rest of the milk in the pan. Put back over a gentle heat and cook, stirring continuously, until the mixture becomes thick. Remove from the heat immediately.

4. Pass the mixture through a sieve into a bowl. Add the butter and stir in to melt. Place a disc of baking parchment or silicone paper directly on the surface of the crème pâtissière to stop a skin forming. Leave to cool and then chill before using.

PAIN AUX RAISINS

MAKES about 24 / PREP 2 hours / BAKE 15–20 minutes

If you're new to making pastries, this classic recipe is an ideal one to start with.

1 quantity Danish pastry dough (see page 173), chilled
Flour for dusting
1 quantity crème pâtissière (see page 174)
225g raisins
1 tsp ground cinnamon
2 medium eggs, beaten
150g apricot jam to glaze

For the lemon icing
200g icing sugar
2 tbsp water
Finely grated zest of 1 lemon

1. Line 3 or 4 baking trays with baking parchment or silicone paper.

2. Cut the rested dough in half. Roll one half out on a lightly floured surface to a large rectangle, about 7mm thick. Turn it 90°, if necessary, so a long edge is facing you. Smear half the crème pâtissière over the dough, leaving a clear 5cm margin along the near edge. Sprinkle half the raisins and cinnamon over the crème. Roll the dough towards you into a sausage ①, keeping it as tight as possible – give a gentle tug each time you roll to tighten the dough and give it a little tension. When you reach the end, roll the sausage back and forth a few times to seal the join. Repeat with the second piece of dough and remaining ingredients.

3. Cut the rolls into 3cm slices ②. Lay cut side up and apart on the baking trays and put each inside a clean plastic bag. Leave to rise at cool room temperature (18–24°C) until at least doubled in size, about 2 hours.

4. Heat your oven to 200°C. Brush the risen pastries with beaten egg and bake for 15–20 minutes until golden brown. Meanwhile, warm the apricot jam with a little water in a pan, then sieve. As you take the pastries out of the oven, brush with the jam and transfer to a wire rack to cool. For the icing, stir the ingredients together until smooth. When the pastries are cooled, drizzle the lemon icing over them.

ALMOND PASTRIES

MAKES 18 / PREP 3 hours / BAKE 15–20 minutes

These wonderfully nutty pastries are one of the simplest to shape, and one of the best. Do bake them to a rich golden brown – a crisp surface really adds to the bite. I love to serve them warm from the oven for breakfast.

1 quantity Danish pastry dough (see page 173), chilled
Flour for dusting
1 quantity frangipane (see page 174)
200g flaked almonds
2 eggs, lightly beaten
150g apricot jam to glaze

For the orange icing (optional)
200g icing sugar
2 tbsp water
Finely grated zest of 1 orange

1. Line 3 baking trays with baking parchment or silicone paper.

2. Cut the rested dough in half. Roll out each half on a lightly floured surface to a 30cm square, about 5mm thick. Trim the edges to neaten, then cut into 10cm squares. Fold the corners of each square into the middle and press down firmly with your finger.

3. Put the pastries onto the prepared baking trays, spacing them apart. Put each tray inside a clean plastic bag and leave to rise at cool room temperature (18–24°C) until at least doubled in size, about 2 hours.

4. Heat your oven to 200°C.

5. Place about 1 tbsp of frangipane in the middle of each risen pastry and sprinkle with flaked almonds. Brush the exposed pastry with beaten egg and bake for 15–20 minutes until risen and golden brown.

6. While the pastries are baking, warm the apricot jam with a little water in a pan, then sieve. As you take the pastries out of the oven, brush them with the apricot jam to glaze and place on a wire rack to cool.

7. For the icing, if required, stir the ingredients together until smooth. When the pastries are slightly cooled, dip a pastry brush into the orange icing and dab it over each them. Serve warm.

RASPBERRY DANISH

MAKES 28 / PREP 3 hours / BAKE 15–20 minutes

Good raspberries have a lovely deep flavour and when they are baked on
a pastry the taste intensifies even further. Enhanced with a drizzle of lemony
icing, these are among my favourite Danish pastries and the recipe is easily
adapted for other fruit (see below).

I quantity Danish
pastry dough (see
page 173), chilled

Flour for dusting

I quantity crème
pâtissière (see
page 174)

250g raspberries,
plus extra to finish
if you like

2 medium eggs, beaten
with a splash of milk

150g apricot jam
to glaze

For the lemon icing

200g icing sugar

2 tbsp water

Finely grated zest of
I lemon

1. Line 4 or 5 baking trays with baking parchment or silicone paper.

2. Roll the rested dough out on a lightly floured surface to a rectangle, just
   over 53 x 30cm and about 7mm thick. Trim the edges to neaten, then
   cut into 7.5cm squares. On each square, make 2.5cm cuts from each
   corner going diagonally almost to the centre (see photograph, page 163),
   so you have 4 triangles. Fold one corner from each triangle into the
   centre to create a star shape (see page 163).

3. Put the stars onto the prepared baking trays, spacing them apart to allow
   room for spreading – 6 pastries per tray is ample. Put each tray inside a
   clean plastic bag and leave to rise at cool room temperature (18–24°C)
   until at least doubled in size, about 2 hours.

4. Heat your oven to 200°C.

5. Put I tbsp of crème pâtissière into the middle of each pastry and top
   with 3 or 4 raspberries. Brush the exposed dough with the beaten egg.
   Bake for 15–20 minutes until golden brown.

6. While the pastries are baking, warm the apricot jam with a little water in
   a pan, then sieve. As you take the Danish pastries out of the oven, brush
   them with the apricot jam to glaze and transfer to a wire rack to cool.
   You can, if you like, add more fresh raspberries at this point too.

7. For the icing, stir the ingredients together until smooth. When the
   pastries are cooled, dip a pastry brush into the lemon icing and dab it
   around the edges of each pastry.

BLUEBERRY DANISH

Use 500g blueberries in place of the raspberries. Press 4 blueberries into
the crème pâtissière on each pastry before baking. Add the remaining
blueberries once the Danish pastries have come out of the oven. Glaze and
ice as above.

APRICOT DANISH

Use 3 x 220g tins apricot halves in place of the raspberries. Drain them
well. Place an apricot half in the centre of each pastry on top of the crème
pâtissière before baking. Glaze and ice the Danish pastries as above.

APPLE DANISH WITH SULTANAS

<small>MAKES 16–20 / PREP 3 hours / BAKE 15–20 minutes</small>

These are a firm favourite of my son Joshua. You can vary the icing by
flavouring it with mandarin, satsuma or lemon zest instead of orange.

**1kg dessert apples,
  peeled, cored
  and chopped**

80ml water

100g sultanas

**1 quantity Danish
  pastry dough (see
  page 173), chilled**

Flour for dusting

2 medium eggs, beaten

For the orange icing (optional)

200g icing sugar

2 tbsp water

**Finely grated zest of
  1 orange**

1. Put the apples and water into a saucepan, bring to a simmer and cook,
   stirring often, for about 10 minutes until the apples are soft but still
   holding their shape. Stir in the sultanas and leave to cool.

2. Line 4 baking trays with baking parchment or silicone paper.

3. Cut the rested dough in half. Roll out one half on a lightly floured
   surface to a rectangle, about 35 x 20cm. Cut in half lengthways to make
   two 10cm wide rectangles. Repeat with the second piece of dough. Spoon
   the cooled apple mixture along the length of each rectangle, leaving the
   edges clear and dry. Brush the long edge closest to you with beaten egg,
   then fold the opposite edge over the apple filling to enclose it in a long,
   thin case of dough. Press the edges of the dough together firmly. Cut
   each strip into 4 or 5 pastries.

4. Place 4 or 5 pastries on each prepared baking tray and put each tray
   inside a clean plastic bag. Leave to rise at cool room temperature
   (18–24°C) until at least doubled in size, about 2 hours.

5. Heat your oven to 200°C.

6. Using a sharp knife, make diagonal slashes on the top of the pastries to
   expose the apple filling. Brush the pastry surface with beaten egg. Bake
   for 15–20 minutes until golden brown. Transfer to a wire rack to cool.

7. For the icing, if required, stir the ingredients together until smooth.
   When the pastries are slightly cooled, brush icing on top of each one.

SUMMER BERRY DANISH

You will need 1 quantity of crème pâtissière (see page 174), 175g raspberries
and 175g quartered strawberries. Roll out the dough as above. Spread a line
of crème pâtissière down the centre of each rectangle. Top with the berries.
Fold, seal and divide as above. Let rise, slash and glaze as above. Sprinkle
with slivered almonds and bake as above. Finish the pastries with a lemon
icing (see page 181).

MANGO AND BANANA DANISH

You will need 1 quantity of crème pâtissière (see page 174), 2 chopped large
bananas and 2 chopped large, ripe mangoes. Roll out the dough as above.
Spread a line of crème pâtissière down the centre of each rectangle. Top
with the banana slices, then the mango. Fold, seal and divide as above. Let
rise, slash, glaze and bake as above. Finish with a lemon or orange icing.

LEMON AND LIME PASTRIES

MAKES 18 / PREP 3 hours / BAKE 15–20 minutes

I just love the freshness of lemon curd and lime icing against the sweet richness of Danish pastry. If you have any lemon curd left over, keep it in the fridge to spread on toast or scones.

1 quantity Danish pastry dough (see page 173), chilled
Flour for dusting
2 eggs, beaten

For the lemon curd
Finely grated zest and juice of 4 lemons
190g caster sugar
100g unsalted butter
3 medium eggs, plus 1 egg yolk

For the lime icing
200g icing sugar
2 tbsp water
Finely grated zest of 2 limes

To finish
Finely grated zest of 1 lime

1. To make the lemon curd, put the lemon zest and juice, sugar and butter in a bowl over a pan of simmering water. Heat gently, stirring, until the butter melts. Take the pan off the heat. Beat the eggs and egg yolk together in a bowl, then whisk them into the warm lemon mixture. Return the pan to the heat. Keeping the heat low, cook gently, stirring, until the mixture thickens; this will take 10–15 minutes. Pass the lemon curd through a sieve into a bowl and leave to cool.

2. Line 3 baking trays with baking parchment or silicone paper.

3. Cut the rested dough in half. Roll out one half on a lightly floured surface to a 30cm square. Trim the edges to neaten. Cut into 9 squares. To shape each pastry, fold the corners of each square into the centre and press down firmly with your finger. Repeat with the second piece of dough to shape another 9 pastries.

4. Put the pastries onto the prepared baking trays and put each inside a clean plastic bag. Leave to rise at cool room temperature (18–24°C) until at least doubled in size, about 2 hours.

5. Heat your oven to 200°C.

6. Press a shallow indentation in the middle of each risen pastry with your fingertips, then spoon in about 1 tbsp of lemon curd. Brush the exposed pastry with beaten egg and bake for 15–20 minutes until golden brown. Transfer to a wire rack to cool.

7. For the icing, stir the ingredients together until smooth. When the pastries are cooled, drizzle the lime icing around the edges. Sprinkle the lime zest on the lemon curd filling. Leave to set for 30 minutes.

BRIOCHE

MAKES I large loaf / PREP IO–II hours / BAKE 20–30 minutes

Brioche is a very rich but amazingly light type of bread. Perfect for breakfast and lovely toasted, it's also good in a bread and butter pudding. Making the dough requires a mixer because a lot of soft butter is incorporated, which turns it into a soft, elastic mess. The dough is then chilled for 7 hours to harden the butter so you can shape the brioche. Orange or lemon zest can be added to the dough, along with the butter, to lend a fresh flavour.

500g strong white
   bread flour, plus
   extra for dusting

7g salt

50g caster sugar

10g instant yeast

140ml warm full-fat
   milk

5 medium eggs

250g unsalted butter,
   softened, plus extra
   for greasing

1. Put the flour into the bowl of a mixer fitted with a dough hook. Add the salt and sugar to one side of the bowl and the yeast to the other. Add the milk and eggs and mix on a slow speed for 2 minutes, then on a medium speed for a further 6–8 minutes, until you have a soft, glossy, elastic dough. Add the softened butter and continue to mix for a further 4–5 minutes, scraping down the bowl periodically to ensure that the butter is thoroughly incorporated. The dough will be very soft.

2. Tip the dough into a plastic bowl, cover and chill overnight or for at least 7 hours, until it is firmed up and you are able to shape it.

3. Grease a 25cm round deep cake tin.

4. Take your brioche dough from the fridge. Tip it onto a lightly floured surface and fold it in on itself a few times to knock out the air. Divide it into 9 equal pieces. Shape each piece into a smooth ball by placing it into a cage formed by your hand and the table and moving your hand around in a circular motion, rotating the ball rapidly. Put 8 balls of dough around the outside of the tin and the final one in the middle.

5. Cover with a clean plastic bag and leave to prove for 2–3 hours, or until the dough has risen to just above the rim of the tin.

6. Heat your oven to 190°C.

7. When the brioche is proved, bake for 20–30 minutes or until a skewer inserted into the centre comes out clean. Bear in mind that the sugar and butter in the dough will make it take on colour before it is actually fully baked. Remove the brioche from the tin and cool on a wire rack. Serve warm or at room temperature.

APPLE BRIOCHE

MAKES 2 tarts, each serves 4 / PREP 2½ hours / BAKE 20–25 minutes

This brioche twist on an apple tart is deliciously rich and sweet — lovely
served warm as a pudding with pouring cream or crème fraîche.

½ quantity brioche
   dough (see page 186),
   chilled

Flour for dusting

I quantity crème
   pâtissière (see
   page 174)

4 dessert apples, cored
   and sliced

50g flaked almonds

I egg, beaten

100g apricot jam
   to glaze

1. Line 2 baking trays with baking parchment or silicone paper.

2. Take your brioche dough from the fridge. Tip it onto a lightly floured
   surface and fold it in on itself a few times to knock out the air. Divide
   the dough into 2 pieces and shape each into a ball. With a rolling pin,
   roll out each ball to a circle, about 23cm in diameter. Place on the
   prepared baking trays and smear each circle of dough with a good layer
   of crème pâtissière, leaving a 2.5cm clear margin around the edge.

3. Cover with a clean plastic bag, making sure the bag doesn't touch the
   crème. Leave to prove for 2 hours.

4. Heat your oven to 200°C.

5. When the brioche is proved, arrange the sliced apples over the crème
   in overlapping circles and scatter over the flaked almonds. Brush the
   exposed dough around the edges with beaten egg. Bake for 20–25
   minutes until the edges of the brioche are golden brown.

6. While the brioche is in the oven, warm the apricot jam in a pan with
   a splash of water for a minute or two, then sieve. As you take the tarts out
   of the oven, brush the top of each with apricot jam to glaze. Serve warm.

BRIOCHE WITH BRIE

MAKES 2 small loaves / PREP 2½ hours / BAKE 15–20 minutes

This is a luxurious, soft, cheese-stuffed bread that you can tear apart at the table. I like to serve it warm, about 15 minutes after it's come out of the oven – it makes a pretty spectacular centrepiece. Use Brie de Meaux if you can – it's a fantastic, traditionally made cheese with lots of character.

1 quantity brioche dough (see page 186), chilled

Flour for dusting

200g Brie (ideally Brie de Meaux)

1 egg, beaten, to glaze

Sesame seeds for sprinkling (optional)

1. Line 2 baking trays with baking parchment or silicone paper.

2. Take your brioche dough from the fridge. Tip it onto a lightly floured surface and fold it in on itself a few times to knock out the air. Divide it into 14 equal pieces. Shape each piece into a smooth ball by placing it into a cage formed by your hand and the table and moving your hand around in a circular motion, rotating the ball rapidly.

3. Cut the Brie into 14 equal pieces. Make a large indentation in each ball and insert a piece of brie, then bring up the edges of the dough around the cheese to trap it. Roll the ball in your hands to seal it. Put one ball in the middle of each baking tray, join side down. Put the remaining balls around the central ones in a flower shape, leaving a small gap between each to allow for rising.

4. Put each tray inside a clean plastic bag and leave to prove for 2 hours.

5. Heat your oven to 190°C.

6. When the brioche is proved, brush the top of each ball with beaten egg. Sprinkle with sesame seeds, if you wish. Bake for 15–20 minutes until the brioche is golden brown. Transfer to a wire rack to cool. Serve warm.

BISCUITS PUDDINGS & CAKES

I'VE OFTEN THOUGHT that it is the bread that comes at the start of a meal and the pudding or cake that comes at the end that have the most impact. These are foods that can have a real wow factor and create a lasting impression, and I suppose it's no accident that these are the areas I've chosen to specialise in!

Ever since I was a boy, I have had a sweet tooth. I still remember how much I enjoyed afternoon teas with my grandparents: the loose tea in a teapot, little plates and forks and the cake — either a fruit cake or an iced creation — taking centre stage on a stand. I have never lost my love of cakes, biscuits and indulgent puddings. This is not just because they are so delicious to eat, it's also the way they generally elicit a gasp, or at least a smile, when they are served, and add a general feeling of *joie de vivre* to any get-together.

There's a real emotional element to this kind of cookery. Sweet recipes are often the ones that are cherished, talked about, and handed down from one generation to another. Those I have chosen to include here are no exception. There are many of my old favourites, as well as recipes gathered from family and friends, which I have since used professionally — everything from deliciously simple biscuits to quite spectacular cakes and soufflés.

MAKING PERFECT CAKES AND PUDDINGS

Naturally, whenever you're making a cake or pudding, you want it to turn out perfectly. The real keys to success are accuracy and taking your time over the preparation. Here are a few tips to help ensure great results:

When buying ingredients, keep to the products you have used before and that you know work well. This will help to ensure consistently good results with your bakes.

Always read a recipe through carefully before you start and make sure you have everything you need.

Weigh your ingredients accurately. This is particularly crucial with cakes and biscuits, to allow the right chemistry to take place between the raising agents, fats and starches in the batter or dough.

Try to keep all your main ingredients at a similar temperature, unless otherwise stated. This makes it easier, for instance, to cream sugar and butter together, and reduces the risk of curdling when you add eggs and flour to a creamed mixture. If your mixture does curdle, add a little flour to the mix and this will 'bring it back'.

When creaming butter and sugar together, do so thoroughly, using an electric hand-held whisk or mixer, or beat with a wooden spoon or balloon whisk, until the mixture is light, soft, fluffy and several shades lighter than it was to start with (see right). Creaming traps lots of air in the mixture, which will make your cake nice and light.

Sift the dry ingredients together before adding them to a batter, to combine and aerate them.

It's important to understand how to fold ingredients together gently when required, to keep air in the mixture. Use a large metal spoon or spatula — something with a thin edge that will cut through the mixture — and take it gently around the outside of the mix, then through the middle, lifting the mixture over itself rather than beating it. Turn the bowl a little and repeat. Keep going until the ingredients are evenly combined, but avoid overmixing.

When baking cakes, do not be tempted to open the oven door until the cake appears to be ready — a sudden influx of cold air as you open the door partway through baking is likely to cause your cake to collapse. And never open the door during the cooking of a soufflé!

BUTTERY SHORTBREAD BISCUITS

MAKES about 20 / PREP 45 minutes / BAKE 20 minutes

With its light, buttery flavour and sugar-crystal sweetness, this shortbread is impossible to resist. You can flavour it if you like, adding a handful of chocolate chips or a sprinkling of finely chopped rosemary or lavender to the dough as you knead it.

225g unsalted butter, softened, plus extra for greasing

110g caster sugar, plus extra for dusting

225g plain flour, plus extra for dusting

110g cornflour

Pinch of salt

1. Lightly butter 2 baking trays, or line with baking parchment.

2. Put the butter and sugar into a large bowl and cream together, using an electric hand-held whisk or wooden spoon, until light and fluffy. Sift the flour and cornflour into the bowl, add the salt and mix together until smoothly combined. Tip the mixture out onto a lightly floured surface and knead to a soft dough.

3. Roll out the dough between 2 pieces of baking parchment to a thickness of 1cm. Prick the dough all over with a fork and cut into triangles or whatever shapes you like, using a knife or biscuit cutter. Re-roll the scraps once to cut more (if you re-roll too many times the dough may start to get greasy). Put the shortbreads on the prepared baking trays and chill for least 30 minutes.

4. Meanwhile, heat your oven to 170°C.

5. Bake the shortbreads for about 20 minutes, until just turning golden brown at the edges. Leave on the baking trays for a few minutes to firm up slightly, then lift the shortbreads onto a wire rack. Dust with sugar and leave to cool. They will keep in an airtight container for 3–4 days.

CYPRIOT ALMOND BISCUITS

MAKES about 25 / PREP 45 minutes / BAKE 20 minutes

In Cyprus, these delicious biscuits are traditionally made around Christmas time and served with the rich, dark coffee of the island. Coated in icing sugar and with a lovely soft centre, they are incredibly moreish and make a great alternative to after-dinner chocolates.

125g flaked almonds, toasted, plus extra to finish

125g unsalted butter, softened, plus extra for greasing

185g caster sugar

2 tbsp brandy

2 tbsp milk

200g plain flour

25g cornflour

Icing sugar for dusting

1. Blitz the 125g flaked almonds briefly in a food processor until coarsely ground — you want them to retain some texture.

2. Using an electric hand-held whisk or mixer, or with a wooden spoon, cream the butter in a large bowl until pale, then slowly add the sugar, creaming as you go, alternating with splashes of the brandy, and then the milk. Keep going until everything is well combined.

3. Gently fold in the coarsely ground almonds, then sift over the flour and cornflour and mix gently. Use your hands to bring the mixture together into a soft dough. Wrap in cling film and chill for 30 minutes.

4. Heat your oven to 160°C. Lightly butter 2 baking trays or line with baking parchment or silicone paper.

5. Take teaspoonfuls of the chilled dough, shape into balls with your hands and put them on the prepared trays. Flatten each a little, leaving some space between the biscuits to allow for spreading. Top each biscuit with a couple of flaked almonds.

6. Bake for 20 minutes or until the biscuits are just firm to the touch but still quite pale. Leave on the baking trays for a few minutes to firm up slightly, then transfer to a wire rack to cool. Dust generously with icing sugar before serving. Stored in an airtight tin, these biscuits will keep for 3–4 days.

GRUYERE BISCUITS

MAKES about 20 / PREP 40 minutes / BAKE 10 minutes

I first tasted these on holiday in the Alps, where they were served with
glasses of chilled Champagne. The biscuits were just the most perfect, salty,
savoury contrast to the light fruity flavour of the wine.

75g plain flour

**Sea salt and freshly
ground black pepper**

**75g cold unsalted
butter, cubed, plus
extra for greasing**

75g Gruyère, grated

1. Sift the flour and a large pinch of salt into a bowl or food processor.
   Add the butter and rub in lightly with your fingertips, or blitz in the
   food processor, until the mixture resembles breadcrumbs. Incorporate
   the cheese, then bring the mixture together with your hands, or briefly
   process to a soft dough. Wrap in cling film and chill for 30 minutes.

2. Heat your oven to 200°C and lightly butter 2 baking sheets or line with
   baking parchment.

3. Put the dough onto a lightly floured surface and roll it out to a 5mm
   thickness. Using a 5cm biscuit cutter, cut out rounds and put them
   on the prepared baking sheets, leaving plenty of room for spreading.

4. Bake for 10 minutes or so, until spread out and lightly browned at the
   edges — watch carefully, because these biscuits colour quickly. Grind
   some salt and pepper over them and leave on the baking trays for a few
   minutes to firm up slightly, then slide onto a wire rack. Leave to cool.
   Store the biscuits between layers of baking parchment in an airtight
   container and they will keep for a couple of days.

CHOCOLATE, PEANUT AND RAISIN CLUSTERS

MAKES about 16 / PREP 15 minutes / BAKE 15 minutes

My son Joshua loves making these with me. The mixture is a satisfyingly
gloopy, chocolatey mess and there is always a rush to lick out the mixing bowl.

200g good-quality
 dark chocolate,
 chopped

60g unsalted butter,
 plus extra for
 greasing

1 tbsp golden syrup

170g caster sugar

1½ tsp natural vanilla
 extract

200g peanuts
 (unsalted), toasted
 and chopped

155g raisins

40g plain flour

2 tbsp unsweetened
 cocoa powder

Icing sugar for dusting

1. Heat your oven to 170°C. Lightly butter 2 baking trays or line with
   baking parchment.

2. Put 80g of the chocolate into a heatproof bowl with the butter, golden
   syrup, sugar and vanilla extract. Set over a pan of simmering water and
   heat gently, stirring from time to time, until the mixture is melted
   and smooth.

3. Mix the remaining chopped chocolate with the peanuts and raisins
   in another bowl. Sift the flour and cocoa together over the mixture and
   stir to combine. Add the melted chocolate mixture and stir everything
   together using a wooden spoon.

4. Form tablespoonfuls of the mixture into little mounds on the baking
   trays, leaving a 4cm gap between each.

5. Bake the biscuits for 15 minutes. They will be very soft when they come
   out of the oven, so leave them on the trays until firm enough to handle,
   then transfer to a wire rack to cool completely. Dust with icing sugar
   before serving. These biscuits will keep in an airtight container for
   2–3 days.

① ② ③

SCONES

MAKES 15 small scones / PREP 20 minutes / BAKE 15 minutes

My recipe is unusual in that it uses bread flour to give the finished scones strength and structure. As long as you don't overwork the dough, the scones will be fluffy and light. To achieve this, I use a technique called 'chaffing' which gently brings the dough together without developing the gluten in the flour too much.

500g strong white
  bread flour, plus
  extra for dusting
80g unsalted butter,
  cut into pieces and
  softened, plus
  extra for greasing
80g caster sugar
2 medium eggs, lightly
  beaten
5 tsp baking powder
250ml full-fat milk

To finish
1 medium egg, beaten
  with a pinch of salt

To serve
Butter or clotted
  cream
Strawberry, raspberry
  or other jam

1. Heat your oven to 220°C. Lightly grease 2 baking trays with butter and line with baking parchment or silicone paper.

2. Put 450g of the flour into a large bowl and add the butter. Rub the flour and butter together with your fingers to create a breadcrumb-like mixture.

3. Add the sugar, eggs and baking powder and use a wooden spoon to turn the mixture gently, making sure you go right down to the bottom to incorporate all the ingredients. Add half the milk and keep turning the mixture gently with the spoon to combine. Then add the remaining milk, a little at a time, and bring everything together to form a very soft, wet dough. You may not need to add all of the milk.

4. Sprinkle most of the remaining flour onto a clean surface. Tip the soft dough out onto it and sprinkle the rest of the flour on top. The mixture will be wet and sticky. Use your hands to fold the dough in half, then turn it 90° and repeat. By folding and turning the mixture in this way, ie 'chaffing', you incorporate the last of the flour and add air. Do this a few times until a smooth dough is formed. If the mixture becomes too sticky, use some extra flour to coat it or your hands to make it more manageable. Be careful not to overwork your dough.

5. Sprinkle a little more flour onto the work surface and the dough, then use a rolling pin to gently roll up from the middle and then down from the middle. Turn the dough 90° and continue to roll and pat it out with your hand until about 2.5cm thick. 'Relax' the dough slightly by lifting the edges and allowing the dough to drop back onto the surface.

6. Using a 7cm pastry cutter dipped in flour to prevent sticking, stamp out rounds (1) and place on the baking trays. Don't twist the cutter, just press firmly, then lift up and press the dough out (2). Once you've cut as many rounds as you can, re-roll the dough to cut more. You can keep doing this, but after re-rolling twice, the scones will be less fluffy.

7. Leave the scones to rest for a few minutes, then brush the tops with the beaten egg mixture to glaze (3). Be careful to glaze only the top of the scones – if it runs down the sides it will stop them rising evenly.

8. Bake for 15 minutes or until the scones are risen and golden brown. Leave to cool, then split the scones and add butter or clotted cream and jam to serve.

WHOLEMEAL SCONES WITH CHEESE

MAKES 8 / PREP 15 minutes / BAKE 15 minutes

These lovely cheesy scones are delicious served still warm from the oven with a slick of butter. They are also good alongside a bowl of soup.

125g self-raising flour

125g wholemeal
   self-raising flour

½ tsp salt

100g Cheddar, grated

150–175ml full-fat
   milk

1 egg, lightly beaten

50g Parmesan, grated

1. Heat your oven to 220°C. Line a baking tray with baking parchment.

2. Put the flours and salt into a large bowl and whisk lightly to combine them. Add the grated Cheddar and stir in, then add most of the milk. Bind the ingredients together, using your hands or a spoon, adding more milk if you need it.

3. Tip the mixture out onto a lightly floured surface and lightly fold it together to form a soft dough. Flatten the dough out with your hands to a rough circle, about 2.5cm thick. Slice into 8 triangular pieces. Put the scones on the prepared baking tray.

4. Brush the top of the scones with beaten egg and scatter with grated Parmesan. Bake for 15 minutes, until risen and golden. Transfer the scones to a wire rack to cool. Eat within 24 hours or freeze.

BLUEBERRY BREAKFAST PANCAKES

MAKES about 25 / PREP 10 minutes / COOK 4–6 minutes per batch

Cooking something in a frying pan isn't technically baking, but I have a serious weakness for pancakes and these are so good that I had to include them. Serve warm with maple syrup and fresh berries, or crisp-fried bacon or sausages, and a strong coffee.

200g self-raising flour

1 tsp baking powder

Pinch of salt

1 medium egg, beaten

300ml full-fat milk

1 tbsp melted butter, plus extra for frying

150g blueberries

A little sunflower oil

Maple syrup to serve

1. Sift the flour, baking powder and salt into a large bowl and mix well. In another bowl, combine the beaten egg with the milk. Make a well in the middle of the dry ingredients and slowly whisk in the milk and egg mixture, until you have a smooth batter. Finally, beat in the melted butter and half of the blueberries.

2. Heat a little butter with a dash of oil in a non-stick frying pan over a medium heat. When hot, cook the pancakes in batches: drop in about 1 tbsp of batter for each pancake (try to keep the amount the same for all of them) and cook for 2–3 minutes on each side or until golden. Repeat until all the batter is used, adding a little more butter and/or oil to the pan if necessary. As the pancakes are cooked, stack them on a warm plate, cover and keep warm.

3. Serve the pancakes as soon as they are all cooked, with the remaining blueberries and maple syrup.

CLAFOUTIS MONIQUE

SERVES 6 / PREP 15 minutes / BAKE 25–30 minutes

I've named this pudding after my wife's godmother Monique, the archetypal
Frenchwoman – elegant, charming and an awesome cook. She lives in
the Champagne region of France with a garden full of fruit trees, and her
clafoutis is always brimming with whichever fruit is in season. This recipe
also works well with blueberries, raspberries, plums and pears.

**Large knob of unsalted
butter for greasing**

75g plain flour

75g caster sugar

300ml full-fat milk

**2 medium eggs,
separated**

2 tbsp Kirsch

**400g ripe black
cherries, pitted**

Icing sugar for dusting

1. Heat your oven to 190°C. Generously butter a 25cm round baking dish.

2. Mix the flour and sugar together in a large bowl. Combine the milk and
   egg yolks in another bowl, then gradually whisk into the flour to make
   a smooth batter. Add the Kirsch.

3. In a separate bowl, whisk the egg whites until stiff, then lightly fold them
   into the batter.

4. Warm the buttered dish in a warming oven or briefly in the heated
   oven. Take out the dish and pour in a little of the batter, then add the
   cherries, arranging them evenly around the dish. Pour on the rest of
   the batter, then immediately bake for 25–30 minutes until the clafoutis
   is puffed up and set.

5. Leave to cool a little, then serve sprinkled with icing sugar. A generous
   dollop of crème fraîche mixed with a little sugar and Kirsch is the
   perfect complement. This clafoutis is also very good cold the next day.

BAKLAVA

MAKES about 25 pieces / PREP 30 minutes / BAKE 25–30 minutes

This is a very simple version of a classic dessert, varieties of which can be found all over the Middle East and North Africa. Filo pastry is tricky and time-consuming to make, so instead I have used ready-made filo, which gives excellent results. I've flavoured the baklava with lemon juice, but you can perfume the syrup with rose water or orange flower water if you prefer.

150g unsalted butter, melted

200g shelled pistachio nuts (unsalted)

250g ready-made filo pastry

For the syrup

250g caster sugar

250ml water

Juice of ½ lemon

1. Heat your oven to 180°C. Brush a 20cm square baking dish with a little of the melted butter. Chop the pistachios finely by hand or blitz them in a food processor.

2. Place a sheet of filo pastry in the bottom of the baking dish and brush with melted butter, folding the pastry to fit the dish if necessary. Place another sheet of pastry on top and brush the surface with melted butter. Repeat this until you have used half of the pastry. Add the chopped pistachios, in a single layer. Layer the remaining filo pastry on top, brushing each layer with melted butter.

3. Once you've brushed the top with melted butter, cut through the layers into diamond shapes using a sharp knife.

4. Bake for 25–30 minutes until the baklava is golden and crisp. Set aside to cool completely.

5. To make the syrup, put the sugar, water and lemon juice into a pan and heat gently, stirring, until the sugar is dissolved. Bring to a simmer and simmer for 15 minutes. Pour the hot syrup over the cooled baklava. Leave to cool before cutting and serving.

BLACKBERRY AND PEAR STRUDEL

SERVES 6 / PREP 30 minutes / BAKE 40 minutes

This is a really lovely recipe that I use in the autumn when pears, apples, plums and blackberries are in abundance. You can use any combination of these fruits, but blackberries and pears is my favourite. I like to serve the strudel warm, with thick clotted cream or homemade vanilla ice cream.

120g unsalted butter

½ tsp natural vanilla extract

3 ripe pears

1 tsp grated orange zest

Juice of ½ lemon

100g blackberries

60g sultanas

50g flaked almonds, toasted

120g caster sugar

5 sheets of filo pastry

120g fresh white breadcrumbs

Icing sugar for dusting

1. Heat your oven to 180°C. Line a baking tray with baking parchment.

2. Gently melt 100g of the butter with the vanilla extract.

3. Peel, core and dice the pears. Melt the remaining butter in a frying pan over a medium heat, add the pears and sauté for 2–3 minutes to soften, then drain. (If your pears are perfectly tender, there is no need to cook them.) Tip the pears into a bowl, leave to cool, then toss with the orange zest, lemon juice, blackberries, sultanas, flaked almonds and sugar.

4. Lay a sheet of filo on a clean tea towel on your work surface. Brush with some of the vanilla butter mixture and sprinkle with one-fifth of the breadcrumbs. Repeat these layers until you have used all the filo pastry and crumbs, saving a little butter to finish.

5. Place the fruit filling along a short edge ① of filo, leaving a 5cm clear border. Fold in the long sides and then gently roll up the strudel from the short edge, using the tea towel to help ②. Place seam side down on the prepared baking tray and brush with butter. Bake for 40 minutes or until golden. Leave to cool slightly, then dust with icing sugar to serve.

PEAR, PECAN AND CHOCOLATE CRUMBLE

SERVES 4–6 / PREP 30 minutes / BAKE 15–20 minutes

I know there is a glut of crumble recipes out there, but this is my personal favourite. With melting nibs of dark chocolate and a cinnamon-scented nutty crumble topping, it's a luxurious treat.

4 ripe pears

2 tbsp maple syrup

½ glass medium white wine

50g plain flour

50g rolled oats

25g caster sugar

½ tsp ground cinnamon

50g cold unsalted butter, cubed, plus extra for greasing

50g pecan nuts, roughly chopped

25g flaked almonds

50g good-quality dark chocolate drops or chopped dark chocolate

1. Heat your oven to 180°C. Butter a 28 x 18cm oval ovenproof dish, or dish with similar dimensions.

2. Peel, halve and core the pears, then cut into thick slices. Put the pear slices into the buttered dish, spreading them evenly, then pour over the maple syrup and wine. Roast in the oven for 10 minutes.

3. Meanwhile, put the flour, oats, sugar, cinnamon and cubed butter into a large bowl and rub together with your fingertips until the mixture forms rough crumbs. Alternatively, you can do this in a food processor, using the pulse button. Stir in the pecans and flaked almonds.

4. Remove the pears from the oven, sprinkle with the chocolate and cover with the crumble topping. Bake for 15–20 minutes, until golden and bubbling. Serve warm with crème fraîche or cream.

WHITE CHOCOLATE PUDDINGS WITH PLUMS

SERVES 6 / PREP 30 minutes / BAKE 30 minutes

These little puds are sweet and delicate and go beautifully with the rich, deep flavour of plums. I like to pour on a little cream too. You could use other fruits – lightly poached cherries, perhaps, or fresh raspberries.

Butter for greasing

50g good-quality white chocolate, broken into pieces

3 medium eggs, separated

100g caster sugar

1 tsp natural vanilla extract

50g ground almonds

25g fresh white breadcrumbs

Icing sugar for dusting

For the plums

300ml red wine

300g caster sugar

1 vanilla pod

3 star anise

250g plums, quartered and stoned

1. Heat your oven to 190°C. Butter 6 darioles or other small pudding moulds.

2. Melt the white chocolate in a heatproof bowl over a pan of gently simmering water. Remove from the heat and let cool slightly.

3. Meanwhile, whisk the egg yolks with 50g of the sugar until the mixture is pale and thick and holds a trail when the beaters are lifted. Fold into the melted chocolate, then fold in the vanilla extract.

4. In a clean bowl, whisk the egg whites until soft peaks form, then add the remaining sugar and whisk again until glossy and holding soft peaks. Fold a third of the whisked egg whites into the white chocolate mixture. Fold the ground almonds and breadcrumbs into the remaining whisked egg white, then fold this into the white chocolate mixture.

5. Spoon the mixture into the prepared moulds – they should be a little over half-full. Stand the moulds in a deep roasting tray and pour hot water into the tray to come halfway up the sides of the moulds. Bake for 30 minutes.

6. Meanwhile, to prepare the plums, put the wine and sugar in a saucepan and heat, stirring, until the sugar is dissolved. Split the vanilla pod open, scrape out the seeds with the tip of a knife and add both the pod and seeds to the red wine syrup together with the star anise. Bring to a simmer and cook for about 10 minutes, until slightly thickened. Add the plums to the syrup and poach for a few minutes or until tender (the time will depend on the ripeness of your plums). Remove from the heat.

7. Turn out the white chocolate puddings onto serving plates and dust with a little icing sugar. Serve with the plums in syrup, and cream if you like.

PASSION FRUIT SOUFFLES

MAKES 6 / PREP 40 minutes / BAKE 10–12 minutes

These light, delicate soufflés have a superb flavour and make a very elegant dessert. Serve them as soon as they come out of the oven, without delay, as they will quickly start to subside. They're surprisingly easy to make.

Melted unsalted butter for greasing

140g caster sugar, plus extra for dusting

6 medium egg whites and 2 egg yolks

300ml passion fruit juice (sieved from 20–25 fruits, or good-quality passion fruit juice/smoothie from a carton)

Icing sugar for dusting

1. Heat your oven to 220°C. Brush 6 deep ramekins with melted butter and dust with caster sugar.

2. In a large bowl, using an electric hand-held whisk, whisk the 2 egg yolks with 70g of the sugar for at least 5 minutes until the mixture is pale and thick and holds a trail when the beaters are lifted.

3. In another clean bowl, whisk the egg whites until they hold soft peaks, then whisk in the remaining 70g sugar.

4. Add 60ml of the passion fruit juice to the egg yolk mixture and mix well. Stir one-third of the whisked whites into the yolk mixture, then carefully fold in the remaining whites.

5. Fill the ramekins almost to the top with the soufflé mixture and run your finger around the edge to lift the mixture away from the side slightly (this helps it to rise evenly). Bake for 10–12 minutes until well risen and golden on top.

6. Immediately dust the soufflés with icing sugar and serve. Use the remaining passion fruit juice as a sauce – I like to break into a soufflé with a spoon and pour passion fruit juice inside.

CARROT AND ALMOND CHEESECAKE

SERVES 6–8 / PREP 30 minutes, plus cooling / BAKE 1½ hours

This is one of my all-time favourite baked cheesecakes. Somewhere between a carrot cake and a creamy cheesecake, it's wonderfully light and, as long as you use fresh young carrots, the flavour is intense and aromatic. Try it for afternoon tea on a sunny summer's day.

50g unsalted butter, softened, plus extra for greasing
50g caster sugar
60g self-raising flour, sifted
1 tsp baking powder
1 medium egg
½ tsp almond extract

For the filling
275g cream cheese or sieved cottage cheese
3 medium eggs, separated
A couple of drops of almond extract
100g caster sugar
4 tbsp ground almonds
Juice of 1 orange
175g young carrots, peeled and finely grated
150ml double cream

To serve
150g crème fraîche
2 tbsp marmalade

1. Heat your oven to 180°C. Thoroughly butter a 20cm round springform cake tin.

2. Beat the butter, sugar, flour, baking powder, egg and almond extract together in a bowl until light and creamy, then spread evenly over the bottom of the cake tin. Bake for about 10 minutes until lightly coloured and just firm. Set aside to cool.

3. Turn the oven down to 150°C.

4. To make the filling, in a large bowl beat the cream cheese with the egg yolks, almond extract, 50g of the sugar, the ground almonds, orange juice, grated carrots and cream.

5. In a clean bowl, whisk the egg whites until stiff, then gradually whisk in the remaining sugar until the mixture is smooth and glossy. Lightly fold into the cheese mixture.

6. Pour the filling onto the cooked base in the tin and bake for 1½ hours or until golden brown, well risen and firm; it should be spongy to the touch. Turn off the oven, leave the door ajar and let the cheesecake cool slowly inside for 1 hour.

7. Carefully release the sides of the tin and lift out the cheesecake. Leave to cool completely.

8. When ready to serve, mix the crème fraîche with the marmalade. Slice the cheesecake and serve each slice with a generous spoonful of the marmalade crème fraîche on the side.

GINGERBREAD WITH STICKY PEARS

SERVES 8 / PREP 30 minutes / BAKE 40–50 minutes

This is a combination of my Nan's recipe for gingerbread and my wife
Alexandra's legendary poached pears. It makes a superb follow-up to
a winter roast.

175ml dark treacle

70g caster sugar

250g unsalted butter,
    plus extra for
    greasing

50g crystallised ginger,
    chopped

50g marmalade

250g plain flour

2 tsp baking powder

4 tsp ground ginger

2 tsp ground
    cinnamon

4 medium eggs

175ml full-fat milk

75g crème fraîche,
    plus extra to serve

For the pears

4 fairly ripe pears

Finely grated zest and
    juice of ½ lemon

500ml Champagne or
    dry white wine

175g light muscovado
    sugar

½ vanilla pod, split
    lengthways

1. Put the treacle, caster sugar, butter, crystallised ginger and marmalade into a saucepan and slowly bring to the boil. Transfer to a large bowl and leave to cool for 30 minutes.

2. Meanwhile, heat your oven to 160°C. Butter a 30 x 20cm baking tin, about 6cm deep, and line with baking parchment.

3. Sift the flour, baking powder and spices into a bowl. In another large bowl, whisk the eggs, milk and crème fraîche together. Pour the warm treacle mix into the egg mixture, whisking constantly, then beat in the dry ingredients.

4. Pour the gingerbread mixture into the prepared baking tin and bake for 40–50 minutes or until a skewer inserted into the middle comes out clean. Leave to cool until warm.

5. Meanwhile, peel, halve and core the pears. Put the lemon zest and juice, Champagne, muscovado sugar and vanilla pod with its seeds into a medium saucepan and heat gently, stirring, to dissolve the sugar. Add the pear halves and simmer for 10–20 minutes or until they are tender (very ripe pears will need less time).

6. Transfer the pears to a bowl with a slotted spoon. Boil the cooking liquid for about 15 minutes until it is reduced by at least half to a sticky, syrupy consistency. Pour the syrup over the pears and leave them to cool to room temperature.

7. Serve the gingerbread warm with the poached pears, a spoonful of crème fraîche and a generous drizzle of the syrup.

MRS POST'S LEMON DRIZZLE CAKE

SERVES 10 / PREP 30 minutes / BAKE 40–45 minutes

This recipe was given to me by Helen Post, an excellent baker and close family friend. The light, citrussy flavour and wonderful texture make it possibly the best lemon drizzle cake I have ever tasted.

75g unsalted butter,
  softened, plus extra
  for greasing
125g caster sugar
150g self-raising flour
1 tsp baking powder
2 medium eggs
1 tbsp lemon curd
2½ tbsp full-fat milk

For the drizzle

Finely grated zest and
  juice of 1 lemon
2 tbsp granulated
  sugar

1. Heat your oven to 180°C. Butter a 1kg loaf tin and line it with baking parchment.

2. Beat the butter and caster sugar together in a large bowl, using an electric hand-held whisk or wooden spoon, until the mixture is very light and fluffy – this can take up to 10 minutes. Add the flour, baking powder, eggs, lemon curd and milk, mixing all the time, until the ingredients are thoroughly combined.

3. Pour the mixture into the prepared loaf tin and bake for 40–45 minutes or until a skewer inserted in the middle of the cake comes out clean.

4. Meanwhile, for the drizzle, mix the lemon zest and juice with the granulated sugar. Pour the lemon drizzle over the hot cake in the tin. Leave to cool completely, then serve.

VICTORIA SPONGE

SERVES 8–10 / PREP 30 minutes / BAKE 25–30 minutes

Victoria sponge is an all-time British classic and although I know it isn't traditional to put cream in the middle, I love it. You can, of course, simply ignore the whipped cream suggestion and just sandwich the sponge layers together with jam. I find the all-in-one mixing method, which avoids the separate creaming, beating and folding-in stages, works very well.

230g plain flour
4 tsp baking powder
Pinch of salt
230g caster sugar
230g unsalted butter,
   softened, plus extra
   for greasing
4 medium eggs

To finish
150ml whipping cream
100g raspberry jam,
   or more if you like
Icing or caster sugar
   for dusting

1. Heat your oven to 180°C. Line the base of two 20cm cake tins with baking parchment and lightly butter the sides.

2. Put the flour, baking powder, salt, sugar, softened butter and eggs into an electric mixer or large bowl. Mix on a low speed, or whisk slowly using an electric hand-held whisk, until all the ingredients are evenly combined; do not overmix as this will tighten the mixture and result in a rubbery texture.

3. Divide the mixture evenly between the prepared cake tins and bake for 25–30 minutes until golden and slightly shrunk from the sides of the tin. Leave the sponges to cool slightly in the tins for about 5 minutes, then transfer from the tins to a wire rack to cool.

4. To assemble, keep the best-looking sponge for the top. Lay the other one, top side down, on a serving plate. Whip the cream until it holds soft peaks. Spread the bottom layer with the raspberry jam, then cover with the whipped cream. Place the other layer of sponge on top. Dust with icing or caster sugar and serve.

MARBLE CAKE

SERVES 8–10 / PREP 30 minutes / BAKE 55–70 minutes

This vanilla-scented cake is a real treat and it looks very impressive.
Serve it ready-sliced so everyone can appreciate the marble pattern.

200g unsalted butter, softened

200g caster sugar

1½ tsp natural vanilla extract

3 large eggs

250g plain flour

3 tsp baking powder

40ml full-fat milk

2 tsp unsweetened cocoa powder

Icing sugar for dusting

1. Heat your oven to 180°C. Line a 1kg loaf tin with baking parchment.

2. In a large bowl, beat the butter, 180g of the sugar and the vanilla extract together until the mixture is light and fluffy. Beat in the eggs, one at a time, then sift the flour and baking powder over the mixture and fold in with 2 tbsp of the milk.

3. Spoon two-thirds of the mixture into the prepared loaf tin – it should three-quarters fill the tin. Sift the cocoa over the remaining third of the mixture and fold in, together with the remaining 20g sugar and the last of the milk.

4. Spoon the chocolate mixture over the cake mixture in the tin (1), then run a fork through both mixtures, gently swirling the two together to create a marbled effect (2).

5. Bake for 55–70 minutes, until the cake shrinks slightly from the sides of the tin and a skewer inserted into the centre comes out clean, testing the cake after 55 minutes. Remove the cake from the tin and leave to cool on a wire rack. Once cooled, dust with icing sugar.

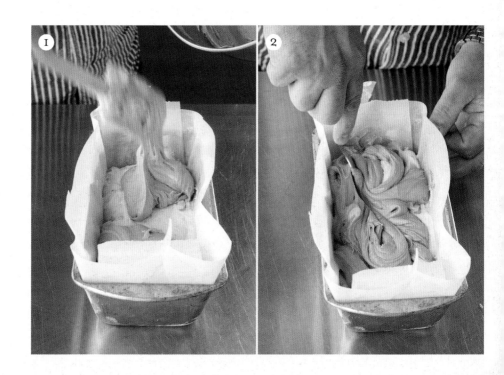

BANANA BREAD WITH WALNUTS

MAKES 1 loaf / PREP 20 minutes / BAKE 40 minutes

Every baker needs a good banana bread recipe up his or her sleeve.
This simple, sustaining loaf is great for packed lunches or picnics.

3 large or 4 medium,
  ripe bananas,
  roughly mashed
250g caster sugar
125g unsalted butter,
  softened
2 medium eggs
250g plain flour
2 tsp baking powder
120g walnut pieces

1. Heat your oven to 190°C. Line a 1kg loaf tin with baking parchment.

2. Using an electric hand-held whisk or mixer, cream the bananas and sugar together until fluffy. Add the butter and beat until evenly combined. Beat in the eggs, one at a time, adding a spoonful of flour with each.

3. Now sift the remaining flour and baking powder over the mixture and carefully fold in. Finally, fold in the walnut pieces.

4. Spoon the mixture into the prepared loaf tin and spread evenly. Bake for 40 minutes, or until a skewer inserted in the centre comes out clean. Remove from the tin and cool on a wire rack.

CHOCOLATE ALMOND CAKE

SERVES 12 / PREP 45 minutes / BAKE 40–45 minutes

I always use Bournville for this cake: I find it has just the right balance of sweetness and cocoa flavour and it's a very stable chocolate that is easy to work with. You can, of course, use a good-quality dark chocolate of your choice, but don't go above about 72 per cent cocoa solids.

Butter for greasing
265g Bournville chocolate, broken into small pieces
6 medium eggs, 5 separated
210g caster sugar
150g ground almonds

For the ganache topping
4 tbsp cherry jam, sieved
120g Bournville chocolate, broken into small pieces
120ml double cream

1. Heat your oven to 180°C. Butter a 20cm round loose-based deep cake tin and line the base with baking parchment.

2. Put the chocolate into a heatproof bowl and set over a pan of hot water. Place the pan over a low heat until the chocolate is melted, stirring occasionally. Allow to cool a little.

3. Whisk the 5 egg whites in a large mixing bowl until stiff but not dry. In a separate large clean bowl, whisk the 5 egg yolks, whole egg and sugar together, using an electric hand-held whisk, until thick and pale; the mixture should be thick enough to leave a trail on the surface when the beaters are lifted.

4. Whisk the ground almonds, melted chocolate and 1 tbsp of the whisked egg whites into the egg yolk mixture. Carefully fold in the remaining egg whites, using a large metal spoon or straight-edged plastic spatula. Turn the mixture into the prepared cake tin.

5. Bake for 40–45 minutes, until the crust that forms on the top is firm and the cake is beginning to shrink away from the sides of the tin. Let the cake cool in the tin for about 10 minutes, then turn it out, upside down, onto a wire rack covered with a tea towel. Peel off the parchment and leave to cool completely, then turn the cake the right way up on the rack, removing the tea towel.

6. Gently heat the jam in a small pan and then brush it evenly over the top and sides of the cake.

7. To make the ganache, put the chocolate into a bowl with the cream and melt slowly over a pan of hot water, stirring occasionally until smooth and glossy. Allow the ganache to cool and thicken slightly (but don't let it set), then pour it onto the centre of the cake and allow it to flow naturally to cover the top and sides; you may need to use a palette knife to spread the ganache around the sides to coat them completely. Leave to set before serving.

SPICED COFFEE AND DATE CAKE

SERVES 8 / PREP 30 minutes / BAKE 35 minutes

I first tried this in Cyprus, where it was made for me by my son's godmother, Auntie Lygia. You will need some good, strong freshly brewed coffee to get the right intensity of flavour.

150g pitted dates,
    halved if large

250ml hot strong
    black coffee

65g unsalted butter,
    melted

120g caster sugar

1 medium egg, beaten

Finely grated zest of
    1 orange

175g plain flour

2 tsp baking powder

1 tsp ground
    cinnamon

½ tsp ground ginger

Generous grating
    of nutmeg

For the topping

45g unsalted butter

90g light muscovado
    sugar

1½ tbsp water

20–30g pecan nuts

1. Heat your oven to 180°C. Line a 20cm round loose-based cake tin with baking parchment.

2. Put the dates and coffee into a bowl and leave to soak for 20 minutes.

3. In a large bowl, beat the melted butter with the caster sugar, egg and orange zest. Drain the dates and add the coffee to the cake mixture.

4. Sift the flour, baking powder and spices together into another bowl and make a well in the centre. Gradually pour in the coffee mixture and beat well to combine, until the mixture is smooth. Pour into the prepared cake tin and arrange the soaked dates on top. Bake for 35 minutes.

5. Meanwhile, prepare the topping. Melt the butter in a pan over a low heat, then stir in the muscovado sugar and heat gently until molten and syrupy. Stir in the water to make a smooth, glossy sauce, then add the pecans and stir to combine.

6. As you take the cake from the oven, pour the topping over the surface, spacing the pecans evenly. Leave to cool in the tin.

TRIPLE LAYER CHOCOLATE CAKE WITH WALNUTS

SERVES 8 / PREP 1 hour / BAKE 45 minutes

Sandwiched together with a delicious chocolate buttercream flavoured with
brandy-soaked sultanas and walnuts, this layer cake is a chocoholic's dream.

175g unsalted butter,
  softened, plus extra
  for greasing
175g caster sugar
3 large eggs
1 tbsp brandy
100g self-raising flour
2 tbsp unsweetened
  cocoa powder
½ tsp baking powder
40g walnuts, chopped
40g digestive biscuits,
  finely crushed

For the filling and topping
75g sultanas
4 tbsp brandy
180–200g good-quality
  dark chocolate
  (about 70 per cent
  cocoa solids or
  Bournville)
150g unsalted butter,
  softened
150g icing sugar,
  sifted, plus extra
  for dusting
50g walnuts, chopped

1. Heat your oven to 180°C. Line a 1kg loaf tin with baking parchment.
   For the filling, soak the sultanas in the brandy in a small bowl.

2. To make the cake, cream the butter and sugar together in a large bowl
   until pale and fluffy; this can take up to 10 minutes. Gradually beat in
   the eggs and brandy, adding a little of the flour with each egg to guard
   against curdling. Sift the remaining flour, cocoa and baking powder
   together over the mixture and fold in gently. Finally, fold in the walnuts
   and biscuit crumbs. Scrape the mixture into the prepared tin.

3. Bake for about 45 minutes or until firm to the touch. Leave in the tin
   for about 10 minutes, then turn out and cool completely on a wire rack.

4. For the filling, chop 150g of the chocolate and melt in a bowl over a pan
   of simmering water. Let cool until barely tepid. In a large bowl, cream
   the butter and icing sugar together, then vigorously beat in the melted
   chocolate until creamy. Add the walnuts and sultanas with their brandy.

5. Slice the cake horizontally ① into 3 layers ②. Use two-thirds of the
   filling to sandwich these together and spread the remaining filling over
   the top of the cake. Grate the rest of the chocolate on top and chill the
   cake thoroughly before serving. Sprinkle with icing sugar to finish.

238 HOW TO BAKE

CARIBBEAN CAKE

This was given to me in Barbados some 25 years ago and I've made it many times since. It's halfway between a cake and a bread – quite dense but still crumbly and melt-in-the-mouth, with a fantastic flavour from the coconut and almonds.

450g plain flour, plus extra for dusting

25g baking powder

185g caster sugar

110g desiccated coconut

80g raisins

70g pecan nuts

50g glacé cherries

20g flaked almonds

110g butter, melted, plus extra for greasing

1 tsp natural vanilla extract

1 tsp almond extract

1 large egg, beaten

100ml water

1. Heat your oven to 150°C. Butter and flour a 1kg loaf tin, or line with baking parchment.

2. In a large bowl, combine the flour, baking powder, 150g of the sugar, 80g of the desiccated coconut, the raisins, pecans, glacé cherries and flaked almonds. Pour in the melted butter and mix well.

3. Combine the vanilla extract, almond extract, beaten egg and water. Add to the flour, fruit and nut mixture and mix until evenly combined. Tip out onto a lightly floured surface and knead the dough lightly for 1 minute.

4. Shape the dough to fit the prepared loaf tin, then place it in the tin. Make a channel, about 4cm wide and 2.5cm deep, along the middle of the dough. Mix together the remaining desiccated coconut and sugar and spoon this mixture into the channel. Close the dough over the filling, patting it to ensure the mixture is sealed in.

5. Bake for about an hour or until risen and golden. Serve warm from the oven, or let the cake cool on a wire rack before serving.

SUMMER FRUIT GENOISE

SERVES 8—10 / PREP 40 minutes / BAKE 25 minutes

A Genoise is a particularly light and delicate kind of sponge, traditionally served with fresh fruit and cream — ideal for tea on a summer's day. This is my favourite way to prepare and serve it.

30g unsalted butter,
    melted

4 medium eggs

125g caster sugar

125g plain flour, plus
    extra for dusting

Pinch of salt

To finish

300g strawberries,
    hulled and halved

2 tbsp icing sugar,
    plus extra for
    dusting

250ml whipping
    cream

250g blueberries

250g raspberries

1. Heat your oven to 180°C. Use a little of the melted butter to grease two 20cm sandwich tins. Dust them lightly inside with flour.

2. Put the eggs and sugar into a heatproof bowl and place over a pan of simmering water. Whisk, using an electric hand-held whisk, for at least 7 minutes until the mixture is trebled in bulk, very pale and thick enough to hold a trail when the beaters are lifted. Sift the flour and salt together over the mixture and fold in gently, keeping in as much air as you can. Finally, very carefully fold in the remaining melted butter.

3. Divide the mixture between the prepared sandwich tins and bake for 25 minutes until golden and slightly shrunk from the sides of the tin. Leave the sponges to cool slightly in the tins for about 5 minutes, then transfer to a wire rack to cool.

4. Meanwhile, put 200g of the strawberries into a blender with 2 tbsp icing sugar and blitz to a smooth purée. It should be intense and sweet; add a little more icing sugar if necessary.

5. Whip the cream until it holds soft peaks. Roughly fold in the strawberry purée, keeping the mixture rippled rather than a uniform pink (or you can simply drizzle the strawberry purée onto the cream as you assemble the cake).

6. Slice each sponge in half horizontally. Lay one of the sponges, cut side up, on a serving plate. Spread a third of the strawberry cream on top, then put a quarter of the blueberries and raspberries around the edge. Add a second layer of sponge and filling, then repeat to create the third layer. Place the final layer of sponge on the top and dust generously with icing sugar.

7. Arrange the remaining strawberries, blueberries and raspberries on top of the cake. Dust lightly with icing sugar and serve.

RASPBERRY AND PASSION FRUIT MUFFINS

MAKES 12 / PREP 20 minutes / BAKE 15–20 minutes

Bursting with sunshine, these are just perfect for that special breakfast or summer afternoon tea. The secret to a good muffin is to avoid overmixing once you add the flour — under- rather than overmix to ensure a light, crumbly texture.

200g unsalted butter, softened

150g caster sugar

4 medium eggs

200g strong white bread flour

1½ tsp baking powder

Pinch of salt

125g passion fruit pulp and seeds (from 3–4 large fruit)

175g raspberries

1. Heat your oven to 200°C. Put 12 paper cases in a muffin tray or line the muffin moulds with scrunched squares of baking parchment.

2. Cream the butter and sugar together in a large bowl until light and fluffy. Beat in the eggs, one at a time. Sift the flour, baking powder and salt together over the mixture and fold in lightly until only just combined; do not overwork. Add the passion fruit pulp and fold in until just combined.

3. Distribute half the muffin mixture evenly between the paper cases, then add a raspberry or two to each. Top with the remaining muffin mix and stud the tops with the remaining raspberries.

4. Bake for 15–20 minutes until the muffins are golden and spring back when gently pressed.

CHERRY CHOCOLATE MUFFINS

MAKES 12 / PREP 20 minutes / BAKE 15–20 minutes

This is a darker and more indulgent variation of my favourite basic muffin recipe. It's perfect for special occasions and particularly good at Christmas.

200g unsalted butter, softened

150g caster sugar

4 medium eggs

200g strong white bread flour

1½ tsp baking powder

Pinch of salt

Splash of milk

150g good-quality dark chocolate, chopped

470g jar pitted morello cherries, drained

1. Heat your oven to 200°C. Put 12 paper cases in a muffin tray or line the muffin moulds with scrunched squares of baking parchment.

2. Cream the butter and sugar together in a large bowl until light and fluffy. Beat in the eggs, one at a time. Sift the flour, baking powder and salt together over the mixture and fold in lightly, with the milk, until only just combined; do not overwork. Add the chocolate and two-thirds of the cherries and fold in, again until just combined.

3. Distribute the mixture evenly between the paper cases and press the remaining cherries into the surface. Bake for 15–20 minutes until the muffins are firm and spring back when gently pressed.

CHOCOLATE BROWNIES WITH DRIED CRANBERRIES

MAKES 16 / PREP 30 minutes / BAKE 25–30 minutes

Tart, tangy little dried cranberries bring a wonderful extra level of flavour
to these rich, intensely chocolatey brownies.

100g unsalted
   butter, cubed

200g Bournville
   chocolate, broken
   into small pieces

4 medium eggs

250g caster sugar

100g plain flour

1 tsp baking powder

30g unsweetened cocoa
   powder

80g dried cranberries

100g walnut pieces

Icing sugar for dusting

1. Heat your oven to 180°C. Line a 20cm square baking tin with baking
   parchment.

2. Put the butter and chocolate into a heatproof bowl and melt together
   over a pan of simmering water. Leave to cool slightly.

3. Using an electric hand-held whisk, whisk the eggs and sugar together
   until the mixture is pale and thick enough to hold a trail when the
   beaters are lifted.

4. Carefully fold the chocolate mixture into the whisked egg mixture. Sift
   the flour, baking powder and cocoa together over the mixture and gently
   fold these in too. Finally, fold in the dried cranberries and walnuts.
   Pour the mixture into the prepared baking tin.

5. Bake for 25–30 minutes until nicely crusted but still soft in the middle.
   Serve warm or cool, sprinkled with icing sugar. For total indulgence,
   have a dollop of cream on the side.

BÛCHE DE NOEL

SERVES 10–12 / PREP 45 minutes, plus cooling / BAKE 12–14 minutes

I have filled this decadent Christmas log with whipped cream and berries
and topped it with a chocolate buttercream icing, but you can both fill and
top it with the chocolate icing if you like, doubling up the quantities.

Vegetable oil for oiling

150g caster sugar

6 large eggs, separated

250g good-quality
   dark chocolate,
   broken into small
   pieces

4 tbsp cold water

For the raspberry cream filling

400ml double cream

250g raspberries

A little Drambuie
   (optional)

For the chocolate buttercream

125g unsalted butter,
   softened

225g icing sugar, plus
   extra for dusting

25g unsweetened cocoa
   powder

1½ tbsp milk

1. Heat your oven to 220°C. Line the base and sides of a 23 x 33cm Swiss roll tin with greaseproof paper and brush the paper lightly with oil.

2. Using an electric hand-held whisk, whisk the caster sugar and egg yolks together in a large bowl until creamy.

3. Put the chocolate and water into a heatproof bowl, set over a pan of gently simmering water and leave until melted and smooth. Let cool slightly, then fold into the whisked mixture.

4. Whisk the egg whites in a clean bowl until stiff but not dry. Gently fold a spoonful of the egg whites into the chocolate mixture to lighten it, then carefully fold in the remaining whites with a large metal spoon (use a gentle action and avoid overmixing). Pour the mixture gently into the prepared tin.

5. Bake for 12–14 minutes (no longer), until the sponge is risen and just firm to the touch. Place the tin on a wire rack and leave the sponge to cool for at least 2 hours.

6. Lay a sheet of greaseproof paper on a board. Once the sponge is cold, with one bold movement, turn it out onto the paper, then lift off the tin. Carefully peel away the paper (1) and trim off any scraggy edges.

7. For the raspberry cream filling, whip the cream until it holds soft peaks. Spread the inverted sponge with the whipped cream, scatter over the raspberries (2) and sprinkle with a little Drambuie, if you like. Roll up from a long side towards you, using the paper to roll; don't worry about the cracks (3). Transfer to a flat serving dish.

8. To make the chocolate buttercream, beat the butter until soft. Sift the icing sugar and cocoa together over the mixture, add the milk and mix to a soft icing. Carefully spread the icing over the cake and mark decoratively with the prongs of a fork. Chill until needed.

9. Sift some icing sugar over the log just before serving. Finish with some festive decorations if you like.

CHRISTMAS CAKE

MAKES at least 16 slices / PREP 1 hour, plus pre-soaking fruit / BAKE 3–3½ hours

This is a classic, richly fruited Christmas cake – deliciously moist and substantial. It tastes wonderful just as it is, but of course the addition of marzipan and snowy white icing make it much more festive and spectacular. You can either make your own marzipan, or use a good-quality bought one. The same goes for the icing.

450g sultanas

225g raisins

225g dried apricots, chopped

115g prunes, chopped

55g glacé pineapple

225g glacé cherries, chopped

225g chopped candied peel

115g blanched almonds, toasted and very roughly chopped

Finely grated zest and juice of 1 orange

70ml brandy

225g unsalted butter, softened

200g light muscovado sugar

5 large eggs

280g plain flour

To finish

2 tbsp apricot jam

1 quantity marzipan (see page 255), or a 500g packet ready-made marzipan

Icing sugar for dusting

1 quantity royal icing (see page 255), or a 500g packet ready-to-roll royal icing

1. Combine all the dried and glacé fruit, candied peel and almonds in a large bowl. Add the orange zest and juice, and the brandy. Mix well, cover and leave for several hours or overnight.

2. Heat your oven to 150°C. Line the base and sides of a 20cm round deep cake tin with a double thickness of baking parchment, cutting it so that it stands a good 5cm proud of the top of the tin.

3. In a very large mixing bowl, beat the butter and sugar together for several minutes until pale and fluffy. Beat in the eggs, one at a time, adding a little of the flour with each to prevent the mixture splitting. Stir in the fruit mixture. Sift the remaining flour over the mixture and fold in, using a large metal spoon. Spoon the mixture into the prepared cake tin and level the surface.

4. Bake in the middle of the oven for 3 hours, then check by inserting a skewer into the centre – if it comes out clean, the cake is cooked. If not, give it a further 15–30 minutes. Leave the cake to cool before removing it from the tin.

5. When your cake is completely cooled – and ideally after a couple of days – you can marzipan and ice it. Warm the apricot jam gently in a saucepan with a splash of water to thin it down, sieve, then brush all over the cake.

6. Roll out 300g of the marzipan to a large circle, about 4mm thick. Using the cake tin as a guide, cut a round of marzipan to fit the top of the cake and position it. Roll out the other 200g marzipan with the trimmings and cut 2 long strips to fit around the side of the cake. Position these, then smooth the marzipan and mould the edges together.

7. If you are using ready-to-roll icing, roll it out on a surface lightly dusted with icing sugar to a thickness of about 5mm. Lift it over the marzipan, smooth down and trim off the excess at the base.

8. If you are using homemade royal icing, smooth it over the cake with a palette knife. You can leave it smooth or swirl it into peaks with the back of a spoon or your palette knife, as you choose. Leave to set.

9. Wrap a ribbon around the side of your Christmas cake and finish as you wish with festive decorations.

ROYAL ICING

MAKES enough for a 20cm round cake / PREP 15 minutes

This is a lovely, whipped-up, snowy icing that is a delight to smooth over
a cake. If you want to get a pure white result, you need to use conventional
white icing sugar, rather than an unrefined or golden variety.

2 large egg whites

**500g icing sugar,
    sifted**

1 tsp glycerine

Squeeze of lemon juice

1. Put the egg whites into a mixing bowl, or the bowl of an electric mixer,
   and start beating. When the egg whites start to look bubbly and frothy
   (but well before they get to a meringue-like stage), start adding the
   icing sugar, a spoonful at a time.

2. When the icing sugar is all incorporated, add the glycerine and lemon
   juice and keep beating until the icing is thick and easily holds peaks.
   It is now ready to use.

MARZIPAN

MAKES 500g / PREP 10 minutes

Making your own marzipan is quick and easy and the result is more subtle
and delicately flavoured than shop-bought versions. This marzipan can be
kept, covered in the fridge, for up to a month.

90g caster sugar

**140g icing sugar, plus
    extra for dusting**

220g ground almonds

**Finely grated zest of
    1 orange**

1 medium egg, beaten

1. Put the caster sugar, icing sugar and ground almonds into a large bowl
   and mix well together. Stir in the orange zest and beaten egg until evenly
   combined and the mixture begins to form a paste.

2. Tip the almond paste onto a work surface lightly dusted with icing sugar
   and knead until it becomes smooth. Wrap in cling film and chill for at
   least 3 hours, or overnight, before use.

WHITE CHRISTMAS CAKE

MAKES at least 18 slices / PREP 1 hour / BAKE 2¼–2¾ hours

This is my mother-in-law's recipe and it makes an excellent alternative to a classic, dark Christmas cake. It is still rich and fruity, but a little lighter and given a lift with plenty of citrus zest as well as a hint of vanilla and almond. It's also jam-packed with nuts. The butter icing is a simple, quick alternative to a traditional royal icing. Give it your personal, artistic finish – I dig out the traditional festive cake decorations that we use every year and leave this to my son.

285g plain flour

½ tsp salt

1 tsp baking powder

½ tsp ground allspice

225g unsalted butter, softened

225g caster sugar

5 large eggs

Finely grated zest of 1 orange

Finely grated zest of 1 lemon

½ tsp natural vanilla extract

½ tsp almond extract

2 tbsp brandy

225g chopped walnuts

110g chopped pecan nuts

225g glacé pineapple

225g glacé cherries

225g chopped mixed peel

110g chopped candied angelica

To finish

2 tbsp apricot jam

1 quantity marzipan (see page 255)

110g unsalted butter, softened

450g icing sugar

5 tbsp brandy

1. Heat your oven to 150°C. Line the base and sides of a 23cm round deep cake tin with a double thickness of baking parchment, cutting it so that it stands a good 5cm proud of the top of the tin.

2. Sift the flour, salt, baking powder and allspice together into a bowl and set aside.

3. In a large bowl, beat the butter until light and fluffy. Add the sugar and beat for several minutes until smooth and light. Beat in the eggs, one at a time, adding 1 tbsp of the flour mix with each to prevent the mixture curdling. Beat in the orange and lemon zest, vanilla extract, almond extract and brandy.

4. Using a large metal spoon, fold in the remaining flour mix, the nuts, glacé fruit, peel and angelica, until thoroughly combined. Spoon into the prepared cake tin and smooth the surface.

5. Bake for 2¼–2¾ hours, until a skewer inserted into the centre of the cake comes out clean. Leave the cake to cool in the tin for 10 minutes, then transfer to a wire rack to cool completely.

6. When your cake is completely cold, warm the apricot jam with a splash of water, sieve and then brush it all over the cake.

7. Roll out 300g of the marzipan to a large circle, about 4mm thick. Using the cake tin as a guide, cut a round of marzipan to fit the top of the cake and position it. Roll out the other 200g marzipan with the trimmings and cut 2 long strips to fit around the side of the cake. Position these, then smooth the marzipan and mould the edges together.

8. To make the icing, beat the butter until smooth and creamy. Beat in half of the icing sugar and stir in the brandy. Beat in the rest of the icing sugar until smooth. Spread the icing evenly over the cake.

SIMNEL CAKE

SERVES 12 / PREP 30 minutes / BAKE 2½ hours

This classic fruit cake is traditionally baked at Easter: the eleven balls of marzipan on top represent Jesus's disciples, minus Judas. There is also a lovely layer of marzipan inside the cake. Homemade marzipan will make it that much more special.

500g marzipan
   (see page 255),
   or use ready-made
225g unsalted butter,
   softened
225g caster sugar
4 medium eggs
225g plain flour
2 tsp ground
   cinnamon
Finely grated zest of
   2 oranges
Finely grated zest of
   2 lemons
225g sultanas
110g currants
110g glacé cherries,
   quartered

To finish
2 tbsp apricot jam
1 egg, beaten

1. Heat your oven to 150°C. Line the base and sides of a 20cm round deep cake tin with baking parchment, cutting it so that it stands a good 5cm proud of the top of the tin.

2. Roll out one-third of the marzipan to about a 5mm thickness and cut a circle that will just fit inside the cake tin. Set aside.

3. Using an electric hand-held whisk or mixer, beat the butter, sugar, eggs, flour, cinnamon, orange zest and lemon zest together in a large bowl until thoroughly blended. Stir in the sultanas, currants and glacé cherries until thoroughly combined.

4. Put half of the mixture into the prepared tin and level the surface. Lay the prepared marzipan circle over the mixture, then spoon the rest of the cake mixture on top and smooth the surface.

5. Bake for about 2½ hours until the cake is well risen and firm to the touch. Leave to cool in the tin for 10 minutes before turning out onto a wire rack to cool completely.

6. When the cake is cooled, warm the apricot jam gently with a splash of water in a small pan over a low heat, sieve, then brush over the top of the cake. Roll out half of the remaining marzipan and cut to fit the top. Press firmly on the top and crimp the edges decoratively. Mark a criss-cross pattern on the marzipan with a sharp knife, if you like.

7. Form the remaining marzipan into 11 balls. Brush the marzipan on the cake with beaten egg, then place the marzipan balls evenly around the edge. Brush the balls with beaten egg too. Use a cook's blowtorch to brown the marzipan balls. Alternatively, do this by putting the cake under a hot grill for a few moments; watch it carefully because the marzipan burns easily.

BRITAIN HAS A STRONG HERITAGE of pies and tarts. My journeys through the country have taken in so many memorable pastry-based recipes, but it was my mother who first introduced me to the world of pies and tarts – her plated apple tarts were a particular treat.

In this chapter I'm going to show you various ways of combining fat with lightly seasoned flour in order to create all sorts of pastries. There is a lot of fear and mystery surrounding this area of baking. I've heard it said that you can either make pastry or you can't. That's nonsense. There is nothing complex or magical about it. As with all baking, you just need to understand the basic chemistry and apply the right, simple techniques. And, once you are confident in your ability to make the different pastries, there are so many wonderful sweet and savoury possibilities.

MAKING YOUR OWN PASTRY

Shortcrust pastry can be made in a food processor, but I prefer to make it by hand. I recommend you do the same, at least once. Rubbing the butter into the flour with your fingertips allows you to get a feel for the way pastry is formed. As you 'rub in' the fat, it coats each grain of flour. This means that, when you add water to bind the dough together, it won't penetrate the flour molecules. Consequently, the gluten stays locked within the flour molecules and is not 'developed', so you end up with a light, crumbly pastry, not a tough, chewy one. Kneading and handling will also develop the gluten in the flour, so working the pastry as little as possible is another way to ensure it stays light and delicate.

Sweet pastry is simply an enriched and sweetened form of shortcrust and the rules for making it are very similar. Again, I prefer to make it by hand, but you can do it in a food processor. It is a very rich and sticky pastry and a little more difficult to roll out. But don't worry, if it crumbles or sticks while you are rolling it, just press it back into a ball and re-roll. You will find it much easier on the second rolling. Chilling sweet pastry thoroughly beforehand is also important in making it easier to handle.

'Baking blind' is essential to add crispiness to your pastry and avoid the dreaded soggy bottom. Begin by rolling out your pastry until it is the same shape as your tart tin and large enough to line it, allowing some excess all the way round. Lift the pastry on the rolling pin and place it over your tin (I). Press the pastry firmly into the corners and sides (2), leaving the excess overhanging the rim of the tin. Prick the base all over with a fork. Line your pastry case with baking parchment, then fill it with a layer of baking beans (3) or dried pasta and bake for 10–12 minutes, depending on the size of your tin. Remove the parchment and beans, brush the pastry case with eggwash (1 egg beaten with a splash of milk) and return to the oven for another 5–8 minutes to dry out the base and seal it. Now trim off the rough edges, using a sharp knife (4).

Puff pastry requires a little bit more commitment than other pastries but it is well worth the effort. When baked, its light, crisp, buttery layers really are exquisite. It's important to roll the dough and butter out neatly to ensure an even result. You also need to allow time for chilling the pastry between rolling and folding to let the butter harden. The quality of the butter you use for puff pastry is crucial. Cheap, poor-quality butters often have a lower melting point and are more likely to leak out of the pastry during baking. I use a good-quality Normandy butter.

You'll also find recipes here using other pastries such as rough puff, and even a traditional hot water crust. The techniques are different, but not complicated, and I urge you to give them a go. They will open up a whole menu of delicious dishes, including the ones I'm sharing here.

SHORTCRUST PASTRY

MAKES enough for a 25cm tart / PREP 10 minutes

The golden rule when making this versatile pastry is not to overwork it.
The less time it takes to make the pastry and bring it together, the more
crumbly and melt-in-the-mouth it will be when cooked. You could make
it in a food processor, but I like to do it by hand as there is far less chance
of overworking it and making it tough. This recipe yields enough for
a standard-sized quiche or tart. You could make double the quantity,
use whatever you need for your specific recipe and freeze the rest. To use
the pastry from the freezer, allow it to come back to fridge temperature
overnight or for at least 7 hours.

**250g plain flour, plus
extra for dusting**

Pinch of salt

**125g chilled unsalted
butter, cubed**

2 medium egg yolks

About 50ml cold water

1. Put the flour and salt into a bowl and mix together, then add the butter
   cubes (1). Rub the ingredients together lightly with your fingertips (2)
   until the mixture looks like breadcrumbs (3).

2. Add the egg yolks (4) and begin to mix with your hands (5), then slowly
   add the water (6) and mix until a paste is formed that leaves the sides of
   the bowl clean (7).

3. Tip the pastry out onto a lightly floured surface and shape into a ball (8).
   Be careful not to overwork or handle it too much. Flatten the pastry
   with your fingers to a disc and wrap in cling film (9). Chill for at least
   3 hours before using.

FLAMICHE

SERVES 8 / PREP I hour / BAKE 30–40 minutes

This tart is a great alternative to a quiche lorraine and the filling has more of a kick. It's a good way to use up leftover cheese from the cheeseboard. I've specified Camembert but Brie, Reblochon, Beaufort or any strong-flavoured white cheese will do just as well.

I quantity shortcrust
  pastry (see page 265)
Butter for greasing
Flour for dusting
I egg, beaten with
  a splash of milk
  (eggwash), for glazing

For the filling
25g unsalted butter
400g leeks, washed
  and sliced
4 medium egg yolks
300ml double cream
Pinch of freshly grated
  nutmeg
Sea salt and freshly
  ground black pepper
150g Camembert or
  other well-flavoured
  cheese

1. Heat your oven to 200°C. Lightly butter a 25cm tart tin.

2. Roll out your shortcrust pastry on a lightly floured surface to a large round (1) page 263, and use to line the prepared tart tin, leaving the excess hanging over the edge (2).

3. Prick the base all over with a fork, line with baking parchment and baking beans (3) and bake blind for 10–12 minutes. Remove the parchment and beans, brush the pastry case with eggwash and return to the oven for another 5–8 minutes to dry out the base and seal it. Trim off the rough edges (4) and set the pastry case aside. Set aside to cool. Lower the oven setting to 180°C.

4. For the filling, melt the butter in a frying pan over a medium-low heat and add the leeks with a pinch of salt. Sauté for 8–10 minutes until the leeks are tender.

5. Put the egg yolks, cream, nutmeg and some salt and pepper into a bowl and beat well. Slice the Camembert lengthways into long, thin strips.

6. Put the cooled pastry case onto a baking sheet and spoon the leeks over the base. Pour the egg mixture over the leeks and fork them up a little, then lay the Camembert strips on top.

7. Bake for 30–40 minutes until just golden and set in the centre. Serve warm, with a light salad and a cold glass of Chablis.

SMOKED SALMON CHEESECAKE WITH LEMON VODKA

SERVES 6 / PREP 30 minutes / BAKE 1¼ hours

I love cheesecakes, and savoury ones are so reminiscent of the 1970s.
For the sake of nostalgia I just had to put one in this book, though with
an updated twist. With its impressive high crust and rich, creamy filling,
this is lovely served in small slices with a fresh green salad.

**1 quantity shortcrust
   pastry (see page 265)**

Butter for greasing

Flour for dusting

**1 egg, beaten with
   a splash of milk
   (eggwash), for glazing**

For the filling

275g cream cheese

**220g smoked salmon,
   chopped**

**3 medium eggs,
   separated**

**Pinch of freshly grated
   nutmeg**

**Finely grated zest and
   juice of ½ lemon**

30g plain flour

**150g soured cream or
   crème fraîche**

2 tsp lemon vodka

150ml full-fat milk

**Sea salt and freshly
   ground black pepper**

Paprika for sprinkling

For the pickled cucumber

**½ large cucumber,
   thinly sliced**

**1 tbsp white wine
   vinegar**

1. Heat your oven to 200°C. Lightly butter a 20cm loose-based deep flan tin or shallow cake tin.

2. Roll out your shortcrust pastry on a lightly floured surface to a large round ① page 263, and use to line the prepared tin, leaving the excess hanging over the edge ②.

3. Prick the base all over with a fork, line with baking parchment and baking beans ③ and bake blind for 10–12 minutes. Remove the parchment and beans, brush the pastry case with eggwash and return to the oven for another 5–8 minutes to dry out the base and seal it. Trim off the rough edges ④ and set the pastry case aside. Set aside to cool. Lower the oven setting to 160°C.

4. To make the filling, put the cream cheese and smoked salmon into a food processor and whiz until evenly combined. Using the pulse button, incorporate the egg yolks, nutmeg, lemon zest and juice, flour, soured cream, vodka, milk and some seasoning (go easy with the salt as the salmon and cheese add plenty). Transfer the mixture to a bowl. Whisk the egg whites in a clean bowl until stiff, then fold them gently into the mixture, using a large metal spoon.

5. Spoon the filling into the prepared pastry case and smooth the surface. Bake for 1¼ hours or until the filling is set and springy to the touch.

6. Meanwhile, prepare the pickled cucumber. Toss the sliced cucumber in a bowl with the wine vinegar and some salt and pepper. Set aside to marinate, turning the cucumber slices from time to time.

7. Once the cheesecake is ready, remove from the oven and leave in the tin for about 10 minutes, then carefully release from the tin and let cool to warm on a wire rack.

8. To serve, drain the pickled cucumber slices and pat dry with kitchen paper. Sprinkle the cheesecake with paprika and serve warm with the pickled cucumber and a green salad on the side.

MOROCCAN PASTIES

MAKES 4 large pasties / PREP 30 minutes / BAKE 40–50 minutes

These lamb and potato pasties are richly spiced with cinnamon, dried chilli
and fresh coriander. I like to serve them with a bowl of yoghurt flavoured
with chopped mint, and some roasted vegetables on the side.

**1 quantity shortcrust
  pastry (see page 265,
  with 1 tsp ground
  turmeric added
  to the flour)**

Flour for dusting

For the filling

200g minced lamb

1 tsp plain flour

**Sea salt and freshly
  ground black pepper**

**1 small red onion,
  peeled and finely
  chopped**

**100g peeled potato or
  sweet potato, diced**

**1 garlic clove, peeled
  and crushed**

**1 tbsp chopped
  coriander leaves**

**½ tsp ground
  cinnamon**

**Pinch of dried chilli
  flakes**

40g butter, cubed

1 egg, beaten

1. Heat your oven to 180°C. Line a baking tray with baking parchment or
   silicone paper.

2. For the filling, put the lamb mince into a bowl with the flour and some
   salt and pepper and mix well with your hands.

3. In another bowl, combine the onion, potato, garlic, coriander,
   cinnamon, chilli flakes and some salt and pepper.

4. Roll out the pastry to about a 3mm thickness and cut four 17cm circles
   using a small plate as a guide.

5. Spoon a quarter of the lamb and a quarter of the vegetables onto one
   half of a pastry circle, leaving a 1cm margin free around the edge. Dot
   the filling with a quarter of the butter. Brush the pastry edge with beaten
   egg, then fold the pastry over the filling to make a pasty. Crimp the edges
   firmly together to seal. Repeat with the rest of the pastry and filling.

6. Put the pasties on the baking tray, brush them with more beaten egg
   and cut a steam hole in the top of each. Bake for 40–50 minutes, until
   golden and bubbling, then leave to cool slightly before serving.

SWEET PASTRY (PATE SUCREE)

MAKES enough for a 25cm tart / PREP 15 minutes

This rich, sweet shortcrust pastry is perfect for classic dessert tarts and pies.
The recipe makes enough for a standard tart. You could make double the
quantity, use whatever you need for your tart or pie and freeze the rest.
To use the pastry from the freezer, bring it back to fridge temperature
overnight or for at least 7 hours. If you prefer, you can use a mixer or food
processor to make the pastry, but take care to avoid overworking.

165g plain flour,
   plus extra for
   dusting

25g ground almonds

120g chilled unsalted
   butter, cubed

55g caster sugar

1 medium egg

1. Stir the flour and ground almonds together in a large bowl, then add
   the butter and rub in with your fingertips (1) until the mixture looks
   like crumbs. Stir in the sugar.

2. Break in the egg (2) and work into the mixture with your fingers,
   bringing it together to form a soft dough.

3. Tip the dough onto a lightly floured work surface and shape it into
   a ball (3). Flatten with your fingers to a disc and wrap in cling film.
   Chill for at least 3 hours before using.

TARTE AUX ABRICOTS

SERVES 8 / PREP I hour / BAKE 20 minutes

When fresh apricots are in season, this is a lovely way to serve them, but it is also very good with tinned apricots. Make sure the pastry is baked to a crisp golden brown crust and leave it to cool completely before filling with the crème pâtissière and fruit.

I quantity sweet pastry (see page 272)

Flour for dusting

I egg, beaten with a splash of milk (eggwash), for glazing

For the crème pâtissière

100g caster sugar

4 medium egg yolks

40g cornflour

500ml full-fat milk

2 vanilla pods

40g butter

2 tbsp Kirsch

For the apricot filling

600g ripe apricots, halved and stoned, or tinned apricots, well drained

To glaze

3 tbsp apricot jam

I tbsp Kirsch

Icing sugar for dusting (optional)

1. First, make the crème pâtissière. Whisk the sugar, egg yolks and cornflour together in a bowl until smoothly combined and set aside. Pour the milk into a large, heavy-based pan. Split the vanilla pods open, scrape out the seeds with the tip of a knife and add these to the milk with the empty pods. Bring to the boil, then remove from the heat.

2. Pour about a quarter of the hot milk onto the egg mixture, whisking as you do so, then return this mixture to the rest of the milk in the pan. Put back over a gentle heat and cook, stirring continuously, until the crème pâtissière becomes thick. Immediately pass through a sieve into a bowl and stir in the butter. Lay a disc of baking parchment directly on the surface to prevent a skin forming. Leave to cool and then chill before using.

3. Roll out your sweet pastry on a lightly floured surface to a large round, about 3mm thick (1) page 263. Don't worry if it crumbles or breaks on the first roll — just press it together and re-roll. Use the pastry to line a 25cm loose-based tart tin, leaving the excess pastry hanging over the edge (2). Chill for 15–30 minutes.

4. Heat your oven to 180°C. Prick the pastry base all over with a fork. Line the pastry case with baking parchment and baking beans (3), and bake blind for 15 minutes. Remove the parchment and beans, brush the pastry case with eggwash and return to the oven for a further 8–10 minutes until the pastry case is cooked and golden brown at the edges. Trim off the rough edges (4) and set the pastry case aside. Leave in the tin for 10 minutes before removing and placing on a wire rack to cool.

5. Beat the 2 tbsp Kirsch into the cooled crème pâtissière and spread it in the cooled pastry case. Arrange the apricots, cut side down, on top.

6. Warm the apricot jam and I tbsp Kirsch in a saucepan until runny, then pass through a sieve. Using a pastry brush, brush this mixture over the apricots to glaze. If you like, you can dust the tart with icing sugar and put it under a hot grill briefly to caramelise the apricots. Serve the tart with vanilla ice cream if you wish.

PECAN AND CHOCOLATE TART

SERVES 12 / PREP 30 minutes / BAKE 40 minutes

Rich, sweet and nutty, this has all the elements of a good old-fashioned treacle tart, but it is far more sophisticated. Serve with a scoop of vanilla ice cream or dollop of whipped cream.

1 quantity sweet pastry (see page 272)

Flour for dusting

For the filling

80g Bournville chocolate, broken into small pieces

45g unsalted butter, cubed

160g granulated sugar

235ml golden syrup

3 medium eggs

1 tsp vanilla extract

235g pecan nuts, chopped

1. Roll out your sweet pastry on a lightly floured surface to a large round, about 3mm thick. Don't worry if it crumbles or breaks on the first roll — just press it together and re-roll. Use the pastry to line a 25cm tart tin and trim off the excess from the edge. Put the pastry case in the fridge to chill while you make the tart filling.

2. For the filling, put the chocolate and butter into a heatproof bowl and place over a pan of simmering water. Leave to melt together, then set aside to cool slightly.

3. In a medium saucepan, combine the sugar and golden syrup. Bring slowly to the boil, stirring constantly. Set aside to cool a little but make sure the mixture remains runny.

4. Beat the eggs together lightly in a large bowl. Add the melted chocolate and butter mixture and whisk until smooth. Now very slowly pour in the hot sugar syrup mixture in a thin trickle, whisking all the time. Keep going until all the syrup is incorporated and the mixture is smooth. Add the vanilla extract and stir in the pecans. Set aside to cool completely.

5. Heat your oven to 180°C. Put the chilled pastry case on a baking tray. Pour the pecan filling into the case and bake for about 40 minutes until the pastry is golden and the filling is set. Leave to cool before serving.

LEMON MERINGUE PIE

SERVES 8 / PREP 1 hour / BAKE 1 hour

This is a good, old-fashioned lemon meringue, with a nice sharp lemon
curd filling and billowing clouds of meringue.

**1 quantity sweet pastry
(see page 272)**

Flour for dusting

**1 egg, beaten with
a splash of milk
(eggwash), for glazing**

For the lemon curd filling

6 large lemons

230g caster sugar

Pinch of salt

80g cornflour

12 medium egg yolks

**230g unsalted butter,
softened**

For the meringue

6 medium egg whites

280g caster sugar

1 tsp cornflour

1 tsp lemon juice

To finish

Icing sugar for dusting

1. Roll out your sweet pastry on a lightly floured surface to a large round,
about 3mm thick ① page 263. Don't worry if it crumbles or breaks on
the first roll – just press it together and re-roll. Use the pastry to line
a 25cm loose-based tart tin, leaving the excess pastry hanging over the
edge ②. Prick the base all over with a fork, then chill the pastry case for
30 minutes.

2. Heat your oven to 180°C. Line the pastry case with baking parchment
and baking beans ③, and bake blind for 15 minutes. Remove the
parchment and beans, brush the pastry case with eggwash and return to
the oven for a further 5–8 minutes until the pastry base is dry and the
edges are just golden. Trim off the rough edges ④ and set the pastry
case aside. Reduce the oven setting to 140°C.

3. To make the lemon filling, finely grate the zest of 2 lemons. Mix the
lemon zest with the sugar, salt and cornflour in a saucepan. Squeeze the
juice from all 6 lemons, strain into the saucepan and beat into the sugar
mixture. Heat gently, stirring often, until thickened. Take off the heat
and beat in the egg yolks, then cook gently again, stirring, until thick.
Remove from the heat and whisk in the butter until melted. Pour the
lemon filling into the baked pastry case.

4. For the meringue, whisk the egg whites in a clean bowl until they hold
soft peaks. Now beat in the sugar, 1 tbsp at a time. When all the sugar
is incorporated, carry on beating for 3–4 minutes until the meringue
is really glossy. Fold in the cornflour and lemon juice. Spoon the
meringue over the lemon filling in the tart.

5. Bake for about an hour, until the meringue topping is crisp and lightly
golden. Leave to cool completely before serving, dusted with icing sugar.

MINCE PIES

MAKES 12 / PREP 30 minutes, plus macerating / BAKE 20 minutes

You just can't beat a classic mince pie, still warm from the oven. I make mine nice and deep in a muffin tin rather than a shallow bun tin, to ensure plenty of filling in every mouthful. If you make your own mincemeat, by all means use it. As here, I often buy a good-quality ready-made mincemeat and enhance it with some lemon zest and added fresh fruit.

I quantity sweet pastry (see page 272)

Butter for greasing

Flour for dusting

I egg, beaten with a splash of milk (eggwash), for glazing

For the filling

410g jar mincemeat

2 satsumas, peeled and segmented, or ½ x 310g tin mandarin orange segments, drained

I dessert apple, unpeeled, cored and finely chopped

Finely grated zest of I lemon

To finish

Caster or icing sugar for sprinkling

1. Put the mincemeat into a bowl. Add the mandarin or satsuma segments, chopped apple and lemon zest. Stir well, cover and leave to macerate for several hours or overnight.

2. Heat your oven to 200°C. Lightly butter a 12-hole muffin tin.

3. Roll out your sweet pastry thinly on a lightly floured surface, to a 2–3mm thickness. Don't worry if the pastry breaks or sticks, just press it together and re-roll. With a 10cm pastry cutter, cut 12 discs and use these to line the muffin tins. Use a 7.5–8cm cutter to cut 12 smaller discs for the pie lids. Re-roll your pastry as necessary to cut enough discs.

4. Put about 2 tsp of the mincemeat into each pastry case. Brush the edges of the smaller discs with eggwash and place over the mincemeat. Press the pastry edges together with your fingertips to seal. Brush the mince pies with a little more eggwash and sprinkle with a little caster sugar. Make a hole in the top of each pie with a small, sharp knife or the tip of a skewer.

5. Bake for about 20 minutes until golden brown and bubbling. Carefully remove the mince pies from the tins and leave on a wire rack to cool. Serve warm or cold, dusted with a little more caster sugar or icing sugar.

PUFF PASTRY

MAKES 600g / PREP 2 hours, plus overnight chilling twice

To ensure success, you need to make sure that both the dough and butter are cold before you put them together – it's even worth chilling the flour. Precision with the initial rolling out of the dough and butter is important, to ensure there are no bits of dough without butter in them. And chilling the pastry between each subsequent roll and fold allows the butter to harden so you can build up clean, even layers of dough and butter.

150g chilled strong white bread flour, plus extra for dusting

150g chilled plain flour

Pinch of salt

2 large eggs

100ml cold water

250g chilled unsalted butter, preferably a good-quality Normandy butter

1. Put the flours, salt, eggs and water into a large bowl and gently mix to an even dough with your fingers. Transfer the dough to a lightly floured surface and knead it for 5–10 minutes until smooth. The dough should feel a little tight at this stage. Shape the dough into a ball and put it into a plastic bag in the fridge to chill overnight, or for at least 7 hours.

2. Flatten the butter into a rectangle, about 40 x 19cm (1), by battering it down with your rolling pin. (You may find this easier to do this if you sandwich the butter between 2 sheets of cling film.) Return to the fridge for an hour to harden the butter again.

3. Roll out your dough to a rectangle, about 60 x 20cm wide. Put the butter on the dough so it covers the bottom two-thirds (2). Make sure that it is positioned neatly and comes almost to the edges.

4. Lift the exposed dough at the top and fold it down over half of the butter (3), then fold the butter-covered bottom half of the dough up over the top (4). You will now have a sandwich of two layers of butter and three of dough (5). Pinch the edges together to seal. Put it back in a plastic bag and chill for 1 hour.

5. Take the dough out of the bag and put it on a lightly floured surface with the short end towards you (6). Roll out to a rectangle as before (7), keeping the edges as even as possible (8). Fold the top quarter down and the bottom quarter up so they meet neatly in the centre. Then fold the dough in half along the centre line. This is called a book turn. Chill in the bag for 1 hour.

6. Take the dough out of the bag, put it on a lightly floured surface with the short end towards you and roll into a rectangle as before. This time, fold down one-third of the dough and then fold up the bottom third to make a neat square. This is called a single turn. Chill in the bag for another hour.

7. Bring your dough out again and do a single turn as previously. Chill in the bag overnight. Your dough is now ready to use (9).

PITHIVIER

SERVES 6–8 / PREP 30 minutes / BAKE 25–30 minutes

The taste of pithivier takes me back to holidays in France. The aroma of warm pastry and baked almonds has me yearning for a slice, along with a grande crème and a seat in the sunshine.

500g puff pastry (see page 283)
Flour for dusting
1 egg, lightly beaten, for glazing

For the filling
140g unsalted butter, softened
140g caster sugar
2 medium eggs, beaten
2 tbsp dark rum
Finely grated zest of 1 small orange
140g ground almonds
20g plain flour

To finish
Icing sugar for dusting

1. Line a baking tray with baking parchment or silicone paper.

2. For the filling, beat the butter and caster sugar together in a large bowl until creamy. Mix in the eggs, rum and orange zest, then fold in the ground almonds and flour.

3. Roll out half of the pastry on a lightly floured surface to a large round, about 3mm thick. Using a large plate as a guide, cut out a 28cm round and put it on the prepared baking tray.

4. Spread the filling over the pastry, leaving a 2cm clear margin around the edge. Brush the pastry edge with some of the beaten egg. Roll out the remaining pastry and cut another 28cm circle. Lay this on top of the filling and press the edges of the pastry firmly together to seal. Chill for at least 1 hour.

5. Heat your oven to 220°C. Brush the pastry with the remaining beaten egg and bake for 25–30 minutes or until golden. Leave to cool, then dust the pie with icing sugar to serve.

PORTUGUESE EGG CUSTARD TARTS

MAKES 12 / PREP 30 minutes / BAKE 25 minutes

These deep-filled tarts encasing a rich, cinnamon-scented custard in
a light, flaky puff pastry are particularly special. The British version uses
sweet pastry and the custard is usually flavoured with nutmeg rather than
cinnamon. I sometimes add a teaspoonful of melted dark chocolate to each
tart before baking, swirling it on top of the custard.

300g puff pastry
  (see page 283)
Butter for greasing
Flour for dusting

For the egg custard filling
90g caster sugar
2 medium egg yolks
  and 1 egg white
20g cornflour
Pinch of salt
350ml full-fat milk
½ vanilla pod, split
1 cinnamon stick
40g unsalted butter

To finish
Icing sugar for dusting

1. First make the custard. Whisk 60g of the sugar, the egg yolks, cornflour
   and salt together in a bowl until smoothly combined, and set aside.
   Put the milk into a large heavy-based pan with the vanilla pod and
   cinnamon stick. Bring to the boil, then remove from the heat. Pour
   about a quarter of the hot milk onto the egg mixture, whisking as you
   do so. Return this mixture to the rest of the milk in the pan.

2. Put back over a gentle heat and cook, stirring continuously, until the
   custard becomes thick. Immediately take off the heat and beat for a
   minute to get rid of any lumps. Pass through a sieve into a bowl. Add
   the butter and stir in to melt. Lay a disc of baking parchment on the
   surface of the custard to stop a skin forming. Leave to cool completely.

3. Lightly butter a 12-hole muffin tin.

4. Roll out your puff pastry on a lightly floured surface to a rectangle,
   about 30 x 20cm. Roll it up like a Swiss roll and cut into 12 equal slices.
   Roll out each piece into a round, large enough to line a muffin mould.
   Gently press into the moulds. Chill for 30 minutes.

5. Heat your oven to 200°C. Line the pastry cases with a square of baking
   parchment and fill with baking beans or pasta to weigh down. Bake
   blind for 8–10 minutes, then remove the paper and beans and return to
   the oven for a couple of minutes to dry the bases. Set aside to cool down.
   Lower the oven setting to 160°C.

6. Whisk the egg white in a clean bowl until stiff peaks form, then gradually
   whisk in the remaining 50g caster sugar. Gently fold this into the cooled
   custard. Pour the custard mixture into the pastry cases to three-quarters
   fill them.

7. Bake for about 25 minutes or until the pastry is cooked and the custard
   is puffed up. Dust with icing sugar before serving.

MOZZARELLA AND BACON BITES

MAKES 18–20 / PREP 20 minutes / BAKE 20 minutes

These little pastry morsels are totally irresistible. Served warm from the oven, they are perfect party food.

500g puff pastry (see page 283)

Flour for dusting

For the filling

Olive oil for cooking

8 rashers of smoked or unsmoked back bacon, rind removed

1 ball of buffalo mozzarella, about 125g, drained

To glaze

1 egg, lightly beaten

1. Heat your oven to 200°C. Line 2 baking trays with baking parchment or silicone paper.

2. Meanwhile, for the filling, heat a little olive oil in a frying pan over a medium heat. Add the bacon and cook gently on both sides until tender. Remove and set aside to cool, then chop into small pieces and set aside.

3. Roll out the puff pastry on a lightly floured surface to a square, about 4mm thick, and then trim to a neat 30cm square. Cut it lengthways into 2 rectangles.

4. Rip the mozzarella into pieces and place down the middle of each rectangle, then scatter over the bacon pieces. Roll up each rectangle to form a sausage and gently roll these to seal the edges. Cut each sausage into 3cm slices.

5. Place the slices, cut side up, on the prepared baking trays. Brush the tops with the beaten egg and bake for about 20 minutes until browned. Serve warm.

COURGETTE TART WITH ROASTED TOMATO COULIS

SERVES 6 / PREP 1 hour / BAKE 20–25 minutes

Colourful and bursting with summer flavours, this fabulous tart originates
from the Loire valley. It's perfect for a picnic or lunch in the garden, with
a crisp white wine.

**250g puff pastry
(see page 283)**

For the topping
**Olive oil for cooking
and sprinkling**
**1 large red onion,
peeled and thinly
sliced**
**Caster sugar for
sprinkling**
**500g courgettes,
thinly sliced**
1 egg, lightly beaten
Squeeze of lemon juice
**Freshly grated
Parmesan**

For the roasted tomato coulis
**About 600g large, ripe
tomatoes, halved**
**3 garlic cloves
(unpeeled)**
**1 tbsp balsamic
vinegar**
Olive oil for drizzling
1 tsp caster sugar
**Sea salt and coarsely
ground black pepper**
**Handful of fresh basil
leaves**

1. First make the coulis. Heat your oven to 220°C. Put the tomatoes,
   cut side up, in a roasting tin. Add the garlic and trickle over the balsamic
   vinegar. Drizzle generously with olive oil. Sprinkle with the sugar and
   season lightly with salt and coarse pepper. Roast for 20–30 minutes or
   until very soft and juicy, and slightly coloured on top (out-of-season
   tomatoes may take longer). Make sure they don't burn. Allow to cool.
   Peel the garlic and put the cloves, along with the tomatoes and any juices
   from the roasting tin, into a blender. Add the basil and a bit more olive
   oil. Blitz thoroughly, then pass through a sieve into a bowl to make
   a smooth sauce. Check the seasoning, cover and chill until needed.

2. Meanwhile, for the topping, heat 1 tbsp olive oil in a frying pan and
   gently fry the onion until softened. Add a sprinkling of sugar and cook
   for another couple of minutes until the sugar is dissolved. Set aside.

3. Plunge the courgette slices into a saucepan of boiling water, blanch for
   a minute or two, then drain, pat dry and leave to cool.

4. Line a baking tray with baking parchment or silicone paper.

5. Roll out your puff pastry on a lightly floured surface to a large circle,
   about 2mm thick. Using a large plate as a guide, cut out a 26cm round.
   Prick all over with a fork and use the tip of a knife to lightly mark a 2cm
   border all round the edge. Place on the prepared baking tray. Chill for
   30 minutes.

6. Heat your oven to 200°C. Spoon the red onion over the pastry within
   the border and then arrange the courgette slices in layers over the top,
   overlapping them slightly. Sprinkle with olive oil and season with salt
   and pepper. Brush the pastry border with beaten egg.

7. Bake for 20–25 minutes until the pastry is puffed and golden brown.
   Allow to cool. Before serving, brush with a little more olive oil and
   squeeze over some lemon juice. Finish with a fine grating of Parmesan
   and a few twists of the pepper mill. Serve with a spoonful of tomato
   coulis on the side and a light summer salad.

SAUSAGE ROLLS

MAKES 6 large rolls / PREP 2 hours, including chilling / BAKE 30 minutes

These mighty meaty rolls are made particularly flavoursome with the addition of a dollop of caramelised onion chutney inside.

For the rough puff pastry

225g plain flour

½ tsp salt

200g chilled unsalted butter, cubed

Juice of ½ lemon

180–200ml cold water

For the filling

450g sausagemeat

1 tbsp chopped thyme

Sea salt and freshly ground black pepper

60g caramelised onion chutney

To glaze

1 egg, lightly beaten

1. To make the pastry, put the flour, salt and butter into a bowl. Stir the lemon juice into the water and add three-quarters of the liquid to the bowl. Gently stir until the mix binds together, adding the remaining water if necessary. You should have a lumpy dough. Do not work or knead the dough too much — you want to keep the lumps of butter.

2. Tip the dough out onto a floured surface and flatten out to a rectangle. Using a rolling pin, roll out slightly to a narrow rectangle, about 2.5cm thick. Fold one-third of the dough up on itself, then the opposite third down over that, as if folding a business letter. This is called a 'turn'. Wrap the pastry in cling film and rest in the fridge for 20 minutes.

3. Unwrap the pastry and repeat the turn by rolling it, at a 90° angle to the original roll, out to a rectangle, about 40 x 15cm. Fold as above, then re-wrap and chill for a further 20 minutes. Repeat the process twice more, chilling the dough for at least 20 minutes between each turn.

4. Heat your oven to 200°C. Line 2 baking trays with baking parchment or silicone paper.

5. Roll out your dough to a rectangle, about 60 x 20cm, and trim the edges to neaten. Cut into 6 even rectangles.

6. For the filling, mix the sausagemeat with the thyme and some salt and pepper. Divide the sausagemeat into 6 portions. Using floured hands, roll each portion into a sausage shape.

7. Spread a teaspoonful of chutney along each pastry rectangle, leaving the edges clear. Lay a filling sausage across the top of each pastry rectangle ①. Roll up to enclose the sausage filling ② and brush the pastry edges with beaten egg to seal.

8. Place the sausage rolls on the prepared baking trays. Brush with beaten egg and cut several diagonal lines across the top each sausage roll. Bake for 30 minutes or until golden brown and cooked through.

PORK PIES

MAKES 12 / PREP 1 hour / BAKE 50 minutes

A proper pork pie is such a great inclusion in a lunchbox or party spread.
These use a traditional hot water crust pastry, and are very easy to make.

For the hot water crust pastry

265g plain flour, plus extra for dusting

55g strong white bread flour

55g unsalted butter, cubed

65g lard

1 tsp salt

135ml boiling water

1 egg, lightly beaten, for glazing

For the filling

1 large onion, peeled and finely chopped

380g pork loin, finely chopped

100g unsmoked back bacon, finely chopped

Small bunch of parsley, leaves only, chopped

Sea salt and freshly ground black pepper

1 large or 2 small sheets of leaf gelatine

½ chicken stock cube

300ml boiling water

1. Heat your oven to 190°C. Have ready a 12-hole muffin tin.

2. First make the pork filling. Put the onion, pork, bacon and parsley into a bowl with some salt and pepper and mix well. To check the seasoning of the mix, fry a tiny nugget of the mixture in a frying pan until cooked through. Leave to cool, then taste and adjust your mixture accordingly. Cover and set aside while you make the pastry.

3. For the hot water crust, put the flours into a bowl. Add the butter and rub in with your fingertips. Heat the lard in a pan until melted. Dissolve the salt in the boiling water, then add to the melted lard. Pour this liquid into the flour. Mix with a spoon then, as soon as it is cool enough, tip the dough onto a lightly floured surface and work together into a ball. Be careful that the dough is not too hot when you start to work it. Once the dough ball is formed, leave it to cool slightly. If it's still lumpy, work it a minute or two longer. Divide the dough in two, making one piece slightly bigger than the other.

4. Working as quickly as you can, roll out the larger piece of dough (1) to about a 3mm thickness; it should be glossy and still warm to touch. Using an 11–12cm cutter, cut out 12 rounds to line the muffin moulds. Put them into the moulds, shaping to fit the sides. The pastry should come slightly above the rim of each mould. Roll out the other piece of dough (2) and use a 6–7cm cutter to cut out 12 lids (3). Lift away the trimmings (4) and re-roll the pastry if you need to cut more, but only once. As it cools, it stiffens and becomes more brittle.

5. Put a heaped tablespoonful of the filling into each pastry case (5). Use a chopstick or something similar to make a good-sized hole, about 5mm in diameter, in the middle of each pie lid (6). Brush the pastry case rims with beaten egg and place the lids on top. Crimp the edges together well to seal (7). Brush the pastry lids with beaten egg (8). Bake the pies for 50 minutes until golden brown.

6. While the pies are in the oven, soften the gelatine in cold water to cover for 5 minutes or so. In a jug, dissolve the chicken stock cube in the boiling water. Drain the gelatine and squeeze to remove excess liquid, then add to the stock and stir until completely dissolved.

7. When the pies come out of the oven, enlarge the holes in the top if necessary, then carefully pour in a little of the gelatine mixture (9). Leave the pies to cool and settle overnight before serving. Or, once cold, chill for a couple of hours.

POACHER'S PIE

SERVES 8 / PREP 45 minutes / COOK 1 hour, 20 minutes

Pies like this were the centrepiece of the dining table in Georgian times.
They look and taste great, can be served hot or cold, and – best of all – they
are easy to make. Here I've used a standard pie dish, but I often make this
pie in an old-fashioned, hinged pie mould that I found in a junk shop –
it's worth looking out for these at car boot fairs and antique stalls; most
good kitchen shops sell a modern equivalent.

For the hot water crust pastry

**265g plain flour, plus
extra for dusting**

**55g strong white bread
flour**

**55g unsalted butter,
cubed**

65g lard

1 tsp salt

135ml boiling water

**1 egg, beaten, for
glazing**

For the filling

175g lean steak, cubed

**100g lean cooked ham,
chopped**

**225–230g cooked
pheasant, pigeon,
partridge or chicken
breast, chopped**

**Sea salt and freshly
ground black pepper**

350g pork sausagemeat

**300ml good-quality
beef stock (not from
a stock cube)**

1. Heat your oven to 220°C. Stand a 1.5 litre capacity pie dish (or a pie mould) on a baking tray.

2. For the filling, combine the steak, ham and game or chicken in a bowl and season with salt and pepper. Cover and place in the fridge while you prepare the pastry.

3. For the hot water crust pastry, put the flours into a bowl. Add the butter and rub in with your fingertips. Heat the lard in a pan until melted. Dissolve the salt in the boiling water, then add to the melted lard. Pour this liquid into the flour. Mix with a spoon then, as soon as it is cool enough, tip the dough onto a lightly floured surface and work together into a ball. Be careful that the dough is not too hot when you start to work it. Once the dough ball is formed, leave it to cool slightly. If it's still lumpy, work it a minute or two longer.

4. Working as quickly as you can, take two-thirds to three-quarters of the pastry (depending on the dimensions of your dish) and roll it out until large enough to line the base and sides of the pie dish (or mould). Lift into the dish (or mould) and press carefully onto the base and sides, leaving a neat 5mm extending above the rim. Season the sausagemeat, then press it into the bottom and sides of the pie. Spoon the other mixed meats evenly on top.

5. Roll out the remaining pastry to make a lid. Damp the edges of the pie with a little beaten egg, then position the lid over the filling. Pinch the edges of the dough together to seal. Continue to work quickly because, as the pastry cools, it stiffens and becomes more brittle. Cut a small slit in the centre of the pie. Brush with more beaten egg.

6. Bake the pie for 20 minutes, until the pastry is golden brown, then turn the oven down to 180°C and cook for a further 1 hour. Poke a skewer through the hole in the top to check whether the filling is tender. If you are using a pie dish, remove the pie from the oven now. If you are using a mould, you can remove the sides, brush the pastry all over with more beaten egg and bake for an extra 20–30 minutes to brown it.

7. Heat the stock to simmering, then pour it into the pie through the slit in the lid. Serve hot, or leave the pie to cool completely and serve with new potatoes, a green salad and chutneys.

ACKNOWLEDGEMENTS

This book could not have been written without the constant support from my wife Alexandra and my son Joshua, who I rely on totally.

A big thank you to my editors Richard Atkinson and Natalie Hunt at Bloomsbury, for making the book what it is. And to Nikki Duffy and Janet Illsley for their patience and skill, to Peter Cassidy for his beautiful photographs, to Faenia Moore and Róisín Nield for their tremendous work at the photoshoots, and to Peter Dawson and Louise Evans for their excellent design work.

Thanks also to Martine Carter and to my agent Geraldine Woods. I am also grateful to Lulu Grimes, Xa Shaw Stewart, Amanda Shipp, Inez Munsch, Jude Drake and Marina Asenjo.

DIRECTORY

For equipment

Nisbets
www.nisbets.co.uk

Bakery Bits
www.bakerybits.co.uk

Lakeland
www.lakeland.co.uk

KitchenAid
www.kitchenaid.co.uk

Kenwood
www.kenwoodworld.com/uk

For flour

Doves Farm
www.dovesfarm.co.uk

Marriage's
www.marriagesmillers.co.uk

Waitrose (own brand organic)
www.waitrose.co.uk

Wright's
www.wrightsflour.co.uk

For yeast

Allinson's easy-bake yeast

Hovis fast-action bread yeast
(both widely available)

INDEX

onions: coriander, olive and onion
bread 99
courgette tart with roasted tomato
coulis 291
orange: apricot couronne 123
carrot and almond cheesecake 222
Christmas cake 252
mince pies 280
orange icing 178, 182
oval loaves 23
ovens: baking cakes 194
bread-making 29

P

pain aux raisins 177
pain de campagne 136
pain au chocolat 170
pancakes, blueberry breakfast 209
paper, lining 28
partridge: poacher's pie 297
passion fruit: passion fruit soufflés
221
raspberry and passion fruit muffins
244
pasties, Moroccan 270
pastries 160–90
almond croissants 169
almond pastries 178
apple Danish with sultanas 182
apricot Danish 181
baklava 213
blackberry and pear strudel 214
blueberry Danish 181
croissants 160, 164–7
freezing 162
ingredients 162
lemon and lime pastries 185
mango and banana Danish 182
mozzarella and bacon bites 288
pain aux raisins 177
pain au chocolat 170
raspberry Danish 181
sausage rolls 292–3
summer berry Danish 182
techniques 162
pastry 262
baking blind 262
hot water crust pastry 294, 297
puff pastry 262, 283
shortcrust pastry 262, 265
sweet pastry (pâte sucrée) 262, 272
pâte sucrée (sweet pastry) 262, 272
peanuts: chocolate, peanut and raisin
clusters 202

pears: blackberry and pear strudel 214
gingerbread with sticky pears 225
Gorgonzola, pear and walnut bakes
95
pear, pecan and chocolate crumble
217
pecan nuts: Caribbean cake 240
pear, pecan and chocolate crumble
217
pecan and chocolate tart 276
pecan loaf 112
spiced coffee and date cake 237
Stilton and pecan twist 108
white Christmas cake 256
peels 28
pheasant: poacher's pie 297
pies 260
lemon meringue pie 279
mince pies 280
Moroccan pasties 270
pithivier 284
poacher's pie 297
pork pies 294
pigeon: poacher's pie 297
pineapple (glacé): Christmas cake 252
white Christmas cake 256
pistachio nuts: baklava 213
pithivier 284
pitta breads 46
plain white flour 11
plaited loaves 24
eight-strand plait 38
three-strand plait 61
plastic bags 28
plastic containers, making sourdough
30
plums, white chocolate puddings with
218
poacher's pie 297
poppy seeds: pumpkin seed sticks with
poppy seeds 83
seeded bread 100
seeded sourdough 139
pork pies 294
Portuguese egg custard tarts 287
potatoes: Moroccan pasties 270
proving baskets 30, 128
proving bread 26
sourdough 128
proving cloths 30
prunes: Christmas cake 252
puddings 192–3
baklava 213
blackberry and pear strudel 214

carrot and almond cheesecake 222
clafoutis Monique 210
gingerbread with sticky pears 225
ingredients 194
lemon meringue pie 279
passion fruit soufflés 221
pear, pecan and chocolate crumble
217
pecan and chocolate tart 276
tarte aux abricots 275
techniques 194
white chocolate puddings with
plums 218
puff pastry 262, 283
pumpkin seeds: pumpkin seed sticks
with poppy seeds 83
seeded bread 100
seeded sourdough 139

R

raisins: apricot couronne 123
Caribbean cake 240
chocolate, peanut and raisin
clusters 202
Christmas cake 252
fruit loaf 115
pain aux raisins 177
raspberries: bûche de Nöel 251
raspberry and passion fruit muffins
244
raspberry Danish 181
summer berry Danish 182
summer fruit Genoise 243
rising: bread-making 19
sourdough 128
rolls: ale bread rolls 62
breakfast rolls 92
crusty dinner rolls 54
Gorgonzola, pear and walnut bakes
95
rosemary and lemon sourdough 152
royal icing 255
rye flour 12
apricot, date and sultana loaf 116
pain de campagne 136
pecan loaf 112
rye bread 73
seeded bread 100

S

salt, bread-making 13
satsumas: mince pies 280
sausagemeat: poacher's pie 297
sausage rolls 292–3

To my wife Alexandra and my son Joshua

First published in Great Britain 2012

Copyright © 2012 by Paul Hollywood
Photography © 2012 by Peter Cassidy

Bloomsbury Publishing Plc
50 Bedford Square
London WC1B 3DP
Bloomsbury Publishing, London, New Dehi, New York and Sydney

A CIP catalogue record for this book is available from the British Library

ISBN 978 1 4088 1949 4

PROJECT EDITOR Janet Illsley
DESIGNERS Peter Dawson, Louise Evans www.gradedesign.com
PHOTOGRAPHER Peter Cassidy
FOOD EDITOR Nikki Duffy
HOME ECONOMIST Faenia Moore
PROPS STYLIST Róisín Nield
INDEXER Hilary Bird

10 9 8 7 6 5 4 3 2

Printed by Mohn Media, Germany

Innovative use of combined heat and power technology when printing this product reduced CO_2 emissions by up to 52% in comparison to conventional methods in Germany.

www.bloomsbury.com/paulhollywood